T0333898

Information 2.0

New models of information production,
distribution and consumption

Every purchase of a Facet book helps to fund
CILIP's advocacy, awareness and accreditation programmes
for information professionals.

Information 2.0

New models of information production, distribution and consumption

SECOND EDITION

Martin De Saulles

© Martin De Saulles 2012, 2015

Published by Facet Publishing
7 Ridgmount Street, London WC1E 7AE
www.facetpublishing.co.uk

Facet Publishing is wholly owned by CILIP: the Chartered Institute of
Library and Information Professionals.

Martin De Saulles has asserted his right under the Copyright, Designs and
Patents Act 1988 to be identified as author of this work.

British Library Cataloguing in Publication Data
A catalogue record for this book is available from the British Library.

ISBN 978-1-78330-009-9

First published 2012
This second edition 2015

Text printed on FSC accredited material.

Typeset from author's files in 10/13 pt Palatino Linotype and Frutiger by
Flagholme Publishing Services
Printed and made in Great Britain by
CPI Group (UK) Ltd, Croydon, CR0 4YY.

Contents

Preface

In my preface to the first edition of this book, I noted that there was a certain irony in the fact that I have attempted to summarize some of the key challenges facing the information sector through the medium of the book. So three years later perhaps it is doubly ironic that this second edition is still being printed on dead trees. With bookshops and libraries closing all around us, does the book have a future as a means for distributing information? Only time will tell what the future holds for the paper book but I would wager that the monograph, in a variety of published outputs, will continue to be a key format for the transfer of ideas and arguments. What is definitely changing is the economics of publishing, with new technologies such as e-books and new forms of self-publishing challenging the established practices of an industry that has been built around the production and sale of physical items. As this book shows, digital formats allow information to flow more freely in ways that bypass many of the traditional bottlenecks and gatekeepers such as printers, bookshops and libraries. This brings an increase in choice of where and how end-users consume information, and novel ways for new entrants such as Google and Amazon to capture value from these new information flows.

My original intention in writing this book was to provide an overview of the digital information landscape and explain the implications of the technological changes for the information industry, from publishers and broadcasters to the information professionals who manage information in all its forms. This second edition updates a lot of the data from the original text, extends sections and adds new sections where innovations in the information world have occurred. It is not possible in a book of this length to detail every aspect of these changes and challenges but I have attempted to summarize their broader implications through the use of real examples and case studies. By providing examples of organizations and individuals that are seizing on the opportunities thrown up by this once-in-a-generation technological shift I hope the reader is able to better understand where we may be going as information consumers and in broader societal changes.

The structure of the book is fairly linear in that each chapter explores aspects of the information life-cycle, including production, distribution, storage and consumption. However, I hope I have been able to show how these stages are closely intertwined within the broader global information ecosystem that is emerging based on the digitization of content in all its forms. One of the key themes that emerges from this book is the way that organizations, public and commercial, are blurring their traditional lines of responsibility. Amazon has moved from simply selling books to offering the hardware and software for reading them. Apple still makes computer hardware but also manages one of the world's leading marketplaces for music and software applications. Google maintains its position as the most popular internet search engine but has also digitized millions of copies of books from leading academic libraries and backed the development of the world's most popular computing platform, Android. At the heart of these changes are the emergence of cheap computing devices for decoding and presenting digital information and a network which allows the bits and bytes to flow freely, for the moment at least, from producer to consumer.

I hope that this book will be of interest to students on information management and publishing courses as well as practitioners who wish to better understand the dynamics that are shaping the industry they work in. Each chapter contains short case studies, which have been chosen to illustrate particular issues and challenges facing the information industry.

While the digital revolution is impacting on everyone who works with information, sometimes negatively, my objective has been to show that the opportunities outweigh the risks for those who take the time to understand what is going on. Information has never been more abundant and accessible so those who know how to manage it for the benefit of others in the digital age will be in great demand. I hope that this book will help you on that journey.

Martin De Saulles

1
Introduction

When a company spends US$300 million and drills through mountains to lay a 827 mile long fibre optic cable between Chicago and New York with the sole purpose of shaving four-thousandths of a second off the time it takes for financial traders to send and receive information you know that not all data is created equal. In 2010 the company Spread Networks completed this feat of engineering, which required the cable to be laid in the straightest line possible between a data centre in the Chicago Mercantile Exchange and another centre in New York's Nasdaq Stock Exchange. Even though it only reduced the data travel time between the two exchanges by .004 of a second, banks were willing to spend tens of millions of pounds to use the new network (Lewis, 2014). Having access to price data before your competitors, even when it is such a minuscule difference, can be worth billions of dollars. While this may be an extreme example it highlights the central position that information holds in economic life in the 20th century and, as we will see in this book, in our social lives as well.

According to Andrade et al. (2014), 90% of the world's information created since humans first scratched images on cave walls was generated in the last two years and is growing at an annual rate of 40%. Turner et al. (2014) calculate that the amount of information created and replicated globally in 2013 was 4.4 zettabytes; that is 4.4 trillion gigabytes, or if stored on DVDs, enough for that pile of discs to reach more than seven times the distance to the moon. By 2020, Turner et al. estimate this will have grown to 44 zettabytes and will present unprecedented challenges for those tasked with managing this information. For the last 50 years we have been told that developed economies are moving beyond their industrial foundations and into a post-industrial information age. These claims by writers and researchers such as Machlup (1962), Toffler (1970), Bell (1973) and Stonier (1983) were based on the observations that work was becoming more information-focused and economies were more reliant on services than industrial outputs. Analysis of the economic statistics since the early 1960s supports these observations with the service sector now accounting for approximately three-quarters of the economic output of the USA and Europe. Accompanying these developments has been the explosion in digital technologies that have transformed the ways we create, distribute and consume information and have made real the claims that we are moving to a society where information is a central component of our working lives.

This book builds on the work of previous writers and considers the implications of some of the most significant changes of the previous 25 years for information professionals and the rapidly changing environment they find themselves in. Just as the invention of the movable type printing press in the 15th century helped transform society through making information more accessible to the masses, so new methods of publishing based around digital tools are shaping our society in the 21st century. For those unwilling to change the way they work these changes present a threat, but for those, information professionals included, who understand the potential of these new digital publishing platforms and the forces that drive them there are enormous benefits. The following chapters will take you through some of the key technologies behind this revolution and explain how they developed, who is using them and what it means for information professionals and society at large. The remainder of this chapter will set the scene for the issues addressed in this book and provide a broader context within which to think about the digital revolution we find ourselves in.

What is information?

While this may seem like a strange question, particularly in a book aimed primarily at those who work with information, it is worth considering, even if only to set the parameters for what is to be considered in future chapters. In one sense, information is everywhere in that we ascribe meanings to the objects and forms around us. Dark clouds could be said to impart information as they warn us of impending rain and similarly the road sign outside a school tells us to slow down as there may be children crossing. The shape and health of our bodies are defined by the information contained in the genetic instructions within our DNA. However, for the purposes of this book we are concerned with the information that is created by humans for education, entertainment and commerce. Before looking in more detail at some of the technologies that are shaping the production of such information it would be useful to clarify some of the terms that are often used, sometimes confusingly, to describe information: data, information and knowledge. Although there is some debate about the meaning of these terms and the boundaries between them, they provide a useful way of thinking about information and its value.

The notion of a knowledge value chain whereby raw data is turned into usable information and, through human application, becomes knowledge emerged in the early 1970s and was the foundation of knowledge management as an area of organizational activity. Henry (1974) developed this idea and was one of the first to make a differentiation between the stages that go into the creation of knowledge. In his model, data is the raw, unstructured output of various activities that on its own has little or no meaning. In a retail setting it might be the data that is produced by supermarket checkouts that lists product codes and prices. This data can be turned into usable information when it is placed into a broader context of the items that the codes refer to, how many items were sold at particular prices and over a specific time period. This is information that store managers can use to work out what products are selling well and the impact that different pricing strategies are having. In Henry's model, knowledge is created when those managers use the information to make decisions about which products to order more of, what price to sell them at, and which products to drop. Knowledge, then, is the application of understanding and previous experience to the information that is presented.

We will return to the notion of knowledge management in the final chapter but at this stage it is important to explain how the term 'information' is used throughout this book. In essence it primarily refers to this middle stage in knowledge creation but in the context of some of the technologies under discussion it could also be said to refer to data in its rawest state. This is particularly true in Chapter 4 where we look at information distribution and the networks that carry the bits and bytes of the information revolution. The data that flows over these pipes and airwaves is binary and, until it is decoded by the devices at the user's end, would make no sense to anyone. With this clarification in mind, let us now consider some of the most significant innovations of the previous 50 years, which have resulted in the upheavals to the information industries and society more generally.

The foundations of the information society

It is really the combination of computing technologies with communication networks that has formed the basis for the digital revolution we are now living in. Chapter 4 explains in some detail how the internet has evolved from its academic and military origins in the 1970s to its present state as a global information network. However, it is worth remembering that the internet was not originally designed as a mass communications system on which billions of individuals and millions of organizations would come to depend. Early proponents of the notion that western economies were morphing into information societies envisaged far more centralized information networks controlled by a combination of the state and private enterprises rather than the almost anarchic network that is the internet.

As we will see in Chapter 4, there are moves by a number of regulators, policy makers and corporate interests to reshape the internet into something more centrally controlled, but for the moment at least we have a relatively open and accessible network. It is this openness, combined with the mass adoption of computing devices, deskbound and portable, that has encouraged the rampant innovation and development of information services since the 1990s. The traditional guardians of our telecommunication networks, companies such as BT, AT&T, Telstra and so on, were far more conservative in their approach to offering any information services beyond simple voice calls. Although these companies are still important in maintaining the infrastructure of the internet, their significance as gatekeepers to electronic information resources is much diminished. The internet has shifted the balance of power to companies such as Google, Facebook and Amazon, which are the new information gatekeepers. In late 2014, Google had a stock market value higher than that of AT&T, BT and Telstra combined. Alongside the rapid rise of information companies has been the growth of companies making the hardware through which we access their services. Personal computers are as much a part of office-based jobs as the desks they sit on, while smart phones and tablets are also becoming essential items for the modern worker.

In some respects the changes wrought by these technological innovations have been, so far at least, less dramatic than futurologists such as Toffler (1970, 1980, 1990) predicted. His predictions that the education system will have disintegrated by the year 2000 and that offices would by now be paperless still seem some way off. However, the more general point that remote access to the world's information would be made possible by mass computing and communications networks has been realized. Never have so many people had access to so much information at their fingertips and the impact of this on societies around the world has hardly begun to be felt. As we shall see throughout this book, not only is access to information making the notion of an information society real, but the ability of individuals to create and share information is changing the structures of many industries, in particular the publishing sector.

The internet as a driver of change

Since 1995 we have gone from a world where there were approximately 10 million internet users to one where over 2 billion people are connected. Billions of e-mails are sent over this network every day and hundreds of millions of people search Google and other search engines for information spread across the plethora of web pages. According to the UK's Office for National Statistics (ONS), in 2014 84% of UK households had a broadband internet connection, while 91% of 16–24-year-olds used social networking services such as Facebook and Twitter (ONS, 2014). The ways that internet services have impacted on how we find information, communicate, collaborate and purchase goods are rippling through society and forcing organizations and entire industries to restructure the ways they work. The music industry is an obvious example with the illegal sharing of MP3 files and the development of legal downloading services such as iTunes making older formats such as the CD and the business models surrounding them obsolete. More recently, music streaming services such as Spotify are threatening that iTunes may go the same way as the CD.

The film industry is facing similar challenges as the internet presents users with a new channel for consuming media, and, via devices such as smart phones and tablets, the opportunity to break free from the television set in the living room. However, although some organizations may see the internet as a threat to their businesses, it has been argued by others that the broader economic benefits to society outweigh any possible disadvantages to particular interests. Consulting firm, McKinsey has estimated that the internet has accounted for more than one-fifth of GDP growth in mature economies from 2005 to 2010, is responsible for creating 2.6 new jobs for every one that is lost and that smaller companies which are heavy users of web technologies grow twice as fast as others (Manyika and Roxburgh, 2011). On a social level, it has been suggested that social media services such as Facebook and Twitter have been enablers for those involved in the Middle East uprisings in 2011, commonly referred to as the Arab Spring. The extent to which such services had a real influence is debatable, but the fact that the Egyptian Government shut down internet access for its citizens in early 2011 indicates the authorities feared how it was being used by those leading the protests (Williams, 2011).

Librarians and other information professionals were among the first to realize the importance of the internet to the provision of information services and the People's Network initiative launched in 2000 to connect every public library in the UK to the network is generally seen as having been a great success. However, in an age when most households have high-speed internet connections, is there a danger that this aspect of their service will become less relevant? This will be considered in later chapters when the issue of information literacy is examined. The flexibility of many information professionals to adapt to new technologies will be crucial here as the democratization of information access throws up new challenges and opportunities to help users navigate their way through the new digital landscape. While early public initiatives in many countries focused on encouraging companies and people to go online and sample the delights of the internet, there is a growing realization that simply providing someone with an internet connection and a computer does not automatically enhance their education. To update and paraphrase the well known commentator on information matters Barbara Quint, Google probably handles more reference enquiries in a day than have all the world's librarians over the last 100 years (Abram, 2007). In a world where most people's starting point for finding information is no longer the library but an internet search engine, the relevance of information professionals to modern life is under question. As we will see throughout this book, the opportunities for those who keep abreast of these changes are considerable. When everyone has access to the same information it will be those who can manipulate it for the competitive advantage of their users who will thrive.

It should be noted that challenges to libraries and the impact of libraries on the publishing industry is not a recent phenomenon. Shapiro and Varian (1999) note that the first circulating libraries in England sprung up in the 18th century when bookstores could not keep up with demand for popular novels and so started renting them out. At the time publishers were concerned that the commercial renting of books would undermine sales and reduce their profits. However, the greater availability of popular books encouraged more people to learn to read and ultimately increased the overall sale of books. As we will see in Chapter 4, similar concerns were and, to an extent, still are expressed by the larger music publishers who have blamed the rise of downloadable music for the decline of their profits. While there may be substance to these concerns, what is often missed, as with book publishers 250 years ago, is that business models change and technology combined with consumer preferences ultimately shape the way industries evolve. Shapiro and Varian point out that the number of frequent readers in England grew from 80,000 in 1800 to over 5 million by 1850. The decline of one industry is often accompanied by the rise of new ones:

> It was the presence of the circulating libraries that killed the old publishing model, but at the same time it created a new business model of mass-market books. The for-profit circulating libraries continued to survive well into the 1950s. What killed them off was not a lack of interest in reading but rather the paperback book – an even cheaper way of providing literature to the masses.
>
> (Shapiro and Varian, 1999)

The rapid rise of e-books and e-book readers such as the Amazon Kindle is seen by many as a threat to traditional book shops and lending libraries, but, as we will see in later chapters, some of these institutions are adapting to this digital platform through extended and enhanced service offerings.

The big challenges of big data

Chapters 2 and 3 explore the new models of information production and the technologies that are being developed and deployed for the storage of the outputs of the data explosion of the 21st century. The exponential growth in data production has required the invention of new terms such as zettabyte and yottabyte to describe the quantities involved. A lot of this information is the result of the computerization of many business processes such as retail sales, product orders and stock control. Chapter 3 looks at the challenges that large retailers such as Walmart and Tesco face in trying to make sense of the data generated by the billions of products they sell to hundreds of millions of people each year. Analysts often refer to this as 'big data' as its storage, manipulation and analysis are pushing the boundaries of computing and information management capabilities. Similarly the move of many services to the internet are also throwing up new data challenges with web analytics becoming a new area for information professionals to move in to. Freely available and easy to use tools such as Google Analytics allow web managers, through the insertion of a few lines of code onto a website, to track how many people are visiting specific pages, how long they are staying, which sites referred them and what search terms they used to get there.

These tools offer immense opportunities to content creators and publishers to understand the behaviour of their consumers in ways that were never possible under traditional publishing platforms such as newspapers, magazines and books. Once a book or newspaper has been sold it is extremely difficult and often expensive for the publisher to know who has bought their content and what they are doing with it. The newsagent and bookshop have stood in between the publisher and reader, preventing any meaningful commercial relationship from developing. Newspaper subscriptions and publishers such as Reader's Digest, which have engaged in direct sales, are attempting to develop those relationships, but have always accounted for a minority of sales. By offering content via the web, publishers, particularly news producers, can bypass the newsagent, and using web analytics software better understand how readers engage with their outputs. There is a potential danger, though, that publishers may be too driven by the data and become less adventurous and creative in the content they commission. Knowing that readers are drawn to particular types of story may encourage more investment in those types of stories at the expense of less popular but possibly important writing.

As well as publishers, any company that sells goods or services now has to be aware of the ways that information can enhance or, in some cases, damage their business. One of the benefits of the internet for consumers has been the way it has broken down the information asymmetry which traditionally existed in many markets. As individual consumers we did not have the resources to compare the prices and features of multiple product offerings from companies and generally had to buy what was on offer in our local retailers. However, in an age when price comparison sites, review sites and e-commerce sites make researching and purchasing products or services the matter of a few clicks from our living rooms, the power has shifted back to us. Many organizations are struggling to operate in a world where information flows are no longer under their control and their customers are able to share their views and voice complaints to an audience of billions.

McKinsey consultants Manyika et al. (2011) argue that the challenges to organizations posed by managing big data are immense but also offer a way for companies and entire economies to profit from a new wave of innovation based around information management. They claim that while the amount of data generated globally is growing at an annual rate of 40% the growth in IT spending is only growing at an average of 5% per annum. A decrease in the costs of IT hardware will help address this imbalance but it also requires new ways of processing and understanding how this information can be used to increase efficiency. Manyika et al. (2011) suggest that an extra 1.5 million data-savvy managers would be needed in the USA alone to take advantage of this information bonanza. In many ways this presents huge opportunities for information professionals if, as the authors believe, information is going to become the battle ground on which companies attain competitive advantage and economies move out of their moribund states triggered by the financial crises of 2008. Despite some of the worst economic predictions not being realized, most developed economies are still suffering from stagnating or fragile growth more than seven years after the collapse of the banking sector.

Although the production of physical goods and services is the foundation of all successful economies, economists and policy makers are increasingly looking to the exploitation of national data assets to spur growth. In Chapter 4 we will see how the opening up of public sector data, particularly in the UK, is part of a strategy to achieve this by allowing commercial organizations to re-use this data in the creation of new information products and services. Mandel (2012) argues that for too long the focus of economists has been on the production and transfer of goods and services at the expense of examining the role of information in economic growth. He points out that by its nature data is neither a product nor a service: 'We live in a world where "data-driven economic activities" – the production, distribution and use of digital information of all types – are the leading edge of economic growth… Big data – the storage, manipulation, and analysis of huge data sets – is changing the way that businesses and governments make decisions' (Mandel, 2012).

While many of the roles involved in making sense of big data will go to those with the mathematical and computing abilities not traditionally associated with library and information professionals, the core skills of organizing information at the heart of information management must surely play a part. Part of the responsibility for helping information professionals capitalize on these new roles will lie with the educational establishments that offer library and information courses. It is important that these courses reflect the changing nature of information work, and at the very least help their students appreciate the implications of these changes to the jobs they will be applying for.

What about the information providers?

As we will see in Chapter 5, innovation and developments in the hardware that people use to access information resources have had a significant impact on the companies that offer information products and services. Alongside this, the rise of the internet as a distribution network for information services and the world wide web as a user-friendly interface to interrogate online databases have allowed new entrants into the marketplace that have been able to make use of a relatively open and widely used platform. This ease of access to information services for users has impacted on the role of many information professionals who for a number of years have been the experts on and gatekeepers to online information access.

Anyone who has used online databases via providers such as Dialog will be aware that it is a very different experience from the simplicity of carrying out an internet search engine like Google. Although Dialog and other information providers have migrated their services to the web, knowing how to select relevant databases and then search them efficiently still requires skill and at least a basic understanding of information retrieval techniques. For some types of search, information aggregators such as Dialog are still essential ports of call for information professionals. If you need access to patent filings, financial records of private companies or scientific research papers, then there are only a handful of paid information services that will suffice. However, other types of information, particularly news-related content, are becoming commoditized as many news publishers offer their stories for free via their websites. This has undermined the news aggregation services offered by

DataStar, LexisNexis, Factiva and others, which have charged users, typically information professionals, to search and retrieve news stories from the world's newspapers. In 2002, Google launched its Google News service by aggregating 4000 news sources from around the world and providing free access via a search interface similar to the Google internet search page. Despite initially being focused on current affairs, in 2006 the company added an archive to the service offering users the ability to search through 200 years of news articles from a variety of sources.

The impact of Google News and other similar services on the traditional paid-for news aggregation services has been significant and companies like LexisNexis and Factiva have to make a strong case to information professionals about why their fees are worth paying. One of their responses has been to offer services that are more closely integrated into the work flows of the organizations that require news information. The days of the information professional presenting a print-out of search results to an end-user and leaving them to decide what to do with it have come to an end. Online information providers of all sorts are developing products that work within established business practices and technologies to create a smoother flow of information provision that attempts to deliver what is needed at the right time and place and in the most useful format. Paul Al-Nakaash, Head of Content Alliances at LexisNexis, recognizes these new pressures and the responses that are required if companies like his are to remain relevant: 'Aggregators must focus on meeting end user needs. It is no longer enough to have information if it is not available to a user at the appropriate time' (Al-Nakaash, 2011).

Factiva, part of the Dow Jones publishing group and a major provider of global information products and services, is also proactively developing new services to meet the challenges facing information aggregators. Its Factiva Publisher product allows organizations to integrate Factiva content with their own internal information, creating a closer integration between relevant internal and external content.

A more recent challenge to traditional information publishers and aggregators comes from the rise of social media and user generated content that bypasses the established publishing chain altogether. In Chapter 4, the commercial value of information generated by social media will be discussed with particular reference to how organizations are using social media tools to monitor their reputations. Some might argue that social media services such as Facebook and Twitter are only concerned with trivial and insignificant issues, but there is evidence, as we will see, that some of the posts and tweets when examined en masse contain nuggets of valuable insight.

New ways of creating information

Although digital technologies and the internet have led to ever-increasing amounts of information being created and companies like Google have made it easier to search for what we want, the same technologies have also resulted in new models of information production. Cheaper and more powerful personal computers, audio and video production tools and the internet as a distribution network have allowed individuals and small companies to build information empires of their own. Podcasting is a good example of a service that brings together different technologies and standards, and which has been taken up by hundreds of thousands of micro-broadcasters, each catering for different audience niches, from beekeeping to yoga. Similarly blogging platforms such as WordPress and Blogger are being used by writers with specialist knowledge to share their expertise with a potential audience of over 2 billion internet users, and in some cases earn a living from their endeavours. Linking podcasting and blogging is the Really Simple Syndication (RSS) web format for pushing out information updates to subscribers, providing a broadcast-like experience to web users.

The implications of these technologies for the publishing and broadcasting sectors are considered in Chapter 2 where examples of new companies which have based their successful and profitable businesses on these platforms are discussed. While large broadcasters and publishers are unlikely to be threatened by the rise of these new upstarts in the short term, it seems possible that over the longer term a network of multiple content producers will develop as it becomes cheaper and easier to build a media business. When you no longer need expensive printing presses or have to buy expensive broadcast licences from regulators and governments, then a more democratic and accessible media landscape may be the result. We are already seeing the signs of this through dramatic falls in newspaper sales and the amount of time many people in households with internet access spend watching mainstream television.

Where do we put all this information?

If, as discussed earlier in this chapter, consultants IDC and McKinsey are correct that the amount of data produced globally will continue to increase rapidly over the coming years, it will be an information management challenge to develop improved technologies for storing it. This will be particularly important where the information takes on an enhanced commercial value to organizations that use it for attaining a competitive advantage. One of the answers is the development of new compression techniques for reducing the amount of space required for storing digital data.

Music fans have benefited from the compression of digital music files with the mass deployment of the MP3 and other audio compression techniques where source files can be reduced by up to 90% of their original size with little discernible loss of quality. This compression coupled with the falling cost of data storage means that in 2014 a US$300 hard drive can be purchased that is capable of storing every digital music track ever recorded. Similar advances have been made with image and video compression that allow the easy storage and sharing of multimedia via smart phones, cameras and tablets. In Chapter 3 some of the ways that commercially valuable information is being stored are examined. These are presenting environmental as well as technological challenges to the hosting companies. Information-intensive companies such as Google and Facebook manage millions of computer servers, which require large amounts of electricity to power and cool them. In some cases, as we will see, the power requirements are being met by building data centres next to hydro-electric power stations with cooling issues being addressed by locating other centres in the Arctic Circle or under mountains.

Why information matters

This book is an attempt to give an overview of some of the most important developments taking place in the production, distribution, storage and consumption of information and what they mean for those who create information, the professionals who manage it and the people who consume it. The following chapters will expand on the themes and issues touched on in this introduction, and through the use of examples and case studies provide the reader with a better understanding of why digital information is transforming the ways we learn, work and play. Once information moves from the analogue realm into the digital sphere, radical and important changes take place. Computing devices are able to make sense of the 0s and 1s and allow the creation of new insights into what they mean and how they might be useful.

Google's book digitization project encapsulates what this transformation can mean for researchers and students around the world. Google estimated that in 2010 there were 130 million unique books across the world, many of them sitting on dusty library shelves inaccessible to those unable physically to visit that library (Jackson, 2010). Google's stated aim is to scan and create digital copies of all those books by 2020 with an estimated 30 million already scanned by early 2013 (Darnton, 2013). Although legal disputes with publishers and authors have slowed the initiative down, it is still one of the most ambitious and important projects of its kind. By creating searchable copies of books that have been out of reach to most people and offering a freely accessible search interface to interrogate their contents, Google is opening up a large part of the world's information heritage to the masses.

While the Google Books project is only one example of the potential of digitized information for stimulating societal change and innovation, it illustrates what is possible when vision and technical capabilities are combined with hard cash. We are entering a perfect storm created by the convergence of low-cost and accessible tools that allow digital information to be accessed, manipulated and shared in ways never before possible. For content creators and information professionals there has never been a more exciting time to be alive.

2

New models of information production

Introduction

In the introductory chapter we saw how the rise of digital technologies has led to an unprecedented growth in the amount of information being created, distributed and consumed. Personal computing devices have allowed digital information to be produced and replicated while the internet has acted as an open platform for its distribution. This chapter considers the impact of new models of information production on existing industries such as newspaper and book publishing as well as new industries that are being created around digital currencies, social media and the connection to the internet of household and wearable technologies such as thermostats and watches. Although the migration of established newspaper publishers to the internet may be seen as an evolutionary development, the creation of new global currencies based on computer algorithms could be argued to be a far more radical and disruptive innovation. Similarly, the mass adoption of wearable fitness devices, which are constantly tracking and reporting our health status, has the potential to revolutionize researchers' understanding of how diseases develop and help users adopt early preventative measures. Perhaps less socially beneficial but of enormous commercial value are the information trails we leave behind whenever we use a search engine, visit a website or share our thoughts and photos over social media services. We may not see much of the information generated by our smart devices and our online behaviour but it is important to understand what these outputs are, who has access to them and what they are doing with it.

This chapter explores these issues and considers some of the key debates around the economics and ethics of these new forms of information production. Economic issues are at the core of debates around the future of news publishing while there is an emerging concern about who owns the data we are generating through our interactions with the digital world and ethical and legal questions around what third parties should be allowed to do with it. Let us begin our exploration of new models of information production by entering the blogosphere and considering the impact blogs are having on magazine and newspaper industries.

Blogs: the state of the blogosphere

Blogging, in all its forms, continues to evolve, but some would argue that it has not lived up to the expectations that many commentators had when blogging platforms first emerged in the early 2000s. Blogging enthusiasts such as Shirky (2008), Scoble and Israel (2006) and King (2010) claimed that blogs as a form of self-publishing for the masses would be transformative to businesses and wider society. Similar to some of the more recent claims that social media platforms have encouraged many of the national uprisings we have seen around the world in recent years, blogs have been seen as opening up public debates away from the restrictions of commercial and state-controlled media.

At its heart a blog is simply a website with the content arranged in the order in which it was created with the most recent entries appearing first. The word blog is an abbreviation of weblog, which was first used in the late 1990s. The appeal of using a blog to post content to the web is its simplicity, with the blogger not requiring any knowledge of HTML coding or the technicalities of hosting a website. One of the first blogging platforms, Blogger, was launched in 1999 and the aspiring blogger now has a range of competing platforms to choose from including WordPress, Tumblr, TypePad and SquareSpace. There is no reliable and precise estimate for the total number of blogs but in July 2014, Tumblr's website reported hosting 194 million blogs (Tumblr, 2014) and WordPress claimed to host over 70 million in early 2014 (Wordpress, 2014). Blogger, the third major blogging platform, has not released any figures for the blogs it hosts but it would not be unreasonable to state that there were over 300 million blogs in mid-2014. However, this number will contain many abandoned blogs that their creators have long forgotten about and which exist in suspended animation in cyberspace.

In the early days of blogging, critics were swift to characterize this new medium as a platform for lonely egotists to tell the world the dreary details of their lives. While there may have been some truth in this view, in the last ten years a number of blogs have emerged as serious contenders to established print media in providing news editorial, entertainment and expert opinion. The Huffington Post in the USA and Guido Fawkes' blog in the UK show how the blogging platform can certainly complement and perhaps even challenge traditional journalism. During this period mainstream media have embraced blogging as a platform for their journalists to extend their commentary and supplement the outputs of newspapers, magazines and broadcasters. In the early days of blogging there was talk that this new medium presented a direct challenge to newspapers and would become a primary source of news for many people, but the situation is more nuanced than one platform simply replacing another. New communication technologies seldom act as a straight replacement for another; television did not replace radio and mobile phones did not supplant fixed telephones, not yet anyway.

Blogging 2.0

While the total number of blogs continues to grow, their use by traditional news publishers as well as new entrants has evolved. Some of the 'blogs' which have appeared on some mainstream news sites bear little resemblance to the original single person efforts of early bloggers. However, a more recent development is the adoption by a number of newspaper publishers of so-called 'live blogging'. As the name suggests, a 'live blog' is a single blog post to which content is added by the author or authors as an event occurs. New additions to the post are typically time stamped providing readers with a feel for how the story is evolving. This makes good use of the immediacy of blog publishing by allowing their journalists to report stories as they unfold rather than waiting hours or even days for the piece to be written up, checked and edited. Wells (2011) shows how mainstream UK newspapers including the *Financial Times*, the *Guardian* and the *Telegraph*, and the BBC, adopted live blogging for their coverage of the Arab Spring demonstrations to good effect with major upswings in the traffic to these websites. While live blogging may be useful for rapidly evolving stories, Wells argues that they may not be appropriate for all types of reporting. Events that carry on for indefinite periods of time, he claims, may result in sprawling live blogs that readers find difficult to navigate.

Some of the strengths of live blogging as a way to engage readers are shown by Thurman and Rodgers (2014) in their analysis of the way news media used the technique to report on the major earthquake off the coast of Japan in March 2011. Many of us will always remember the shocking images as the tsunami devastated the eastern coast of Japan with massive loss of life and damage to property, including the Fukushima nuclear power plant. Thurman and Rodgers have carried out extensive analysis of the ways news media used live blogging to report the story as it developed and show that website traffic to live blogs was significantly higher than more traditional reporting of the disaster on other parts of the same websites. The researchers also show that reader engagement was higher with visitors spending more time on the live blog. These differences are partly explained by user demand for immediate reporting of rapidly changing events but, as Thurman and Rodgers explain, it is also because live blogs allow the easy inclusion of user generated content. As smart phones become the norm in developed economies the ability of all of us to capture images and video of what we see around us and upload them to media sharing services such as Twitter, Facebook and YouTube vastly increases the number of 'reporters' in the field. Live blogs allow news teams to bring much of this content together without the restrictions of waiting for a staff reporter to get to the scene and file a story.

Firmstone and Coleman's (2014) study into how a local UK council communicates and interacts with its citizens via traditional and new media complements the work of Thurman and Rodgers and shows a news media in a state of transition. Their research into Leeds City Council and the way it interacts with established local media as well as non-traditional online spaces such as social media and blogs indicates the potential for a more engaged electorate. However, the authors argue that those struggling most with this transition are journalists in established local media and the local government communication officers they traditionally deal with. This type of research is important because it presents a more nuanced and sophisticated understanding of the impact of new technologies on the news sector than some of the more binary predictions that new, interactive media will replace broadcast media.

Who can you trust?

Reader trust is a vital prerequisite for any new publisher and something which is very difficult for an unknown blogger to develop. Despite some of the recent phone tapping scandals surrounding the UK's popular press, many of us still prefer to go to generally trusted online sources such as the BBC, the *Guardian* or the *New York Times* to get our news. By incorporating user generated content and combining that with their own reporters' accounts perhaps we are able to have the best of both worlds. There is a tension in this emerging media landscape with 'citizen journalists' often not receiving credit for their reports and mainstream journalists feeling threatened as non-professionals begin to encroach on their territory. Wardle, Dubberley and Brown's (2014) analysis of the ways mainstream media use user generated content revealed that 72% of this content was not labelled or described as such. This, they believe, is partly because of a lack of training in how to use such content but also because an increasing amount of user generated content is being aggregated by established news agencies and then sold on to newsrooms. The assumption among many journalists and editors is that user generated video content is agency footage and so does not require attribution. A major concern here is that if professional journalists do not know or check where footage has originated from, how can we as news consumers trust the authenticity of what we are seeing? If Wardle, Dubberley and Brown are correct then there is work to be done in educating news teams about the appropriate use of user generated content.

Blogs and social media as agents of change

In an era when anyone with an internet connection can be a journalist, commentator and publisher, it is not surprising that many see the emergence of blogs and social media as tools for social change. Spreading messages to a mass audience before the rise of these tools was impossible unless you owned a newspaper, radio or television station. It has been argued that the social uprisings in Iran, North Africa and parts of the Middle East in recent years have taken hold partly because of the easy availability of social media tools to help organize demonstrations and aid coordinated action. Commenting on the Iranian protests by citizens against their election results, Sullivan (2009) was particularly enthusiastic about what he saw as the implications of the rise of social media: 'You cannot stop people any longer. You cannot control them any longer. They can bypass your established media; they can broadcast to one another; they can organize as never before' (Sullivan, 2009).

In a similar vein, Howard et al. (2011) claim that their research at the University of Washington showed that although social media did not cause the uprisings of the Arab Spring, they did empower citizens in a way that allowed them to challenge established and powerful institutions. To many commentators this view has become the perceived wisdom with talk of a 'Twitter Revolution' and a 'Facebook Revolution'. However, not everyone shares this positive, rather technologically deterministic, view. Morozov (2011) is critical of those he sees as being blinded by the potential of social media and who ignore the, often less exciting, reality of the impact which these new technologies are having. Writing about the then UK Prime Minister Gordon Brown's comments that atrocities such as Rwanda could never happen again because the free flow of information would alert the public to such events, Morozov bitingly comments: 'On Brown's logic, the millions who poured into the streets of London, New York, Rome and other cities on February 15, 2003, to protest against the impending onset of the Iraq War made one silly mistake: they didn't blog enough about it. That would have definitely prevented the bloodbath' (Morozov, 2011, 4).

While Morozov may be a little cruel to Gordon Brown's arguably naïve view of the power of technology, he reminds us that we should consider the evidence before becoming too hubristic in our claims.

Blogging for money

Apart from the co-option of blogging technologies and platforms by traditional news media, the other main development has been the commercialization of this publishing platform. Many early bloggers with a commercial bent quickly discovered that simply placing advertisements on their sites was no guarantee of making money. As any for-profit publisher will tell you, monetizing your written assets requires both scale and scope in relation to the audience you hope to attract. Unless you have sufficient traffic to your site then the actual number of people who will click on advertisements will be negligible. Content produced for specific audiences is also important to attract relevant advertisers in a world of commoditized information. Blogs and online sites that achieve these objectives can be particularly profitable.

Although the more reflective, personal diary-types of blogs may be less popular than they once were, blogs catering to more niche interests have become more pervasive. UK-based communications agency Mason Williams (2014) claims from its research on 1200 bloggers across Europe that 65% of them earn money from their blogs with 27% relying on them as their main income stream. These figures are probably not typical of all blogs currently in use but demonstrate that dedicated bloggers can make money. Rao (2014) claims that fashion bloggers with large followings can earn hundreds of thousands of pounds a year as their audience is attractive to brands wishing to associate themselves with the trust and authority that these writers have built up.

However, this authority can also quickly be eroded unless strict dividing lines are drawn between advertising and editorial. Traditional news media have known this for a long time and usually make clear which of their content is paid for by advertisers and which is their own. Legislation exists in most developed economies to enforce this separation. While not subject to this legislation, which is aimed at print and broadcast media, Google has adopted this practice with the advertisements that appear alongside its labelled search results. Not all bloggers and online publishers are quite so ethical in making this dividing line clear, however. Leonhard (2014) points to evidence that Microsoft has been offering influential bloggers money to promote its web browser, Internet Explorer. Sullivan (2012a) shows that Google engaged in similar practices two years earlier when it paid bloggers to promote its Chrome browser via sponsored posts. While this may not raise undue concern if the posts are clearly labelled 'Sponsored by Google' another issue arises, as Sullivan suggests, when some of these posts seem to rank highly in Google search results. The potential conflict of interest for Google is obvious when it controls the world's most popular search engine and has other products and services it would like to promote through content that appears via its search engine. Ethical issues aside, the commercial value of popular niche blogs was demonstrated in 2010 when the large internet media company AOL paid an estimated US$25–40 million for the technology-focused blog TechCrunch (Carlson, 2010). Although large sums like this are not common, this illustrates the potential of this new form of information production for new entrants to the publishing sector.

The economics of print media

Producing newspapers and magazines is an expensive business and the market they operate in is viciously competitive. It is also becoming harder to make a profit as a print publisher, with sales of newspapers falling in many developed economies for several decades and new pressures emerging from the internet where many people do not expect to pay for their news. Graham and Hill (2009) outline some of the key challenges facing the newspaper industry and describe the approaches taken by publishers of regional newspapers to adapt to this new world of news. To better understand these challenges it is important to appreciate the key stages in the production of a newspaper. The value chain of printed news production is shown in Figure 2.1, which sets out the chain's main processes, actors, costs and revenues.

Figure 2.1 illustrates the range of costs that go into the production of a newspaper before it reaches the reader. Employing journalists, photographers and editors, buying printing presses and the ink and paper they require, and then delivering the printed copies around the country to retailers and readers before breakfast is a costly and complicated enterprise. Unsold copies of a daily

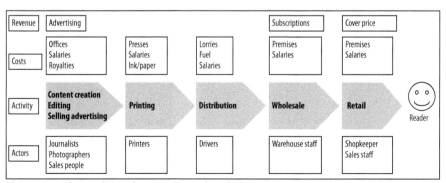

Figure 2.1 The traditional newspaper value chain

newspaper are worthless by
the evening when the process
of printing the next day's
papers has already begun. The
appeal to a publisher of using
the internet as a way to circumvent some of the processes
is obvious. Figure 2.2 illustrates the more streamlined
value chain of a news blog.

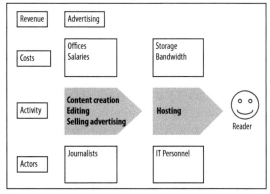

Figure 2.2 The value chain of a news blog

The impact on the cost
structure of stripping out the
printing and distribution of a
newspaper varies between publishers but it is possible it could save up to 60%
of total costs (OECD, 2010). Jarvis, a veteran of print media and a prominent
blogger, is critical of the approach taken by many news publishers in dealing
with the internet and, slightly tongue in cheek, makes an ecological case for
moving news online:

> Casting off atoms will allow newspapers to brag: no more dead trees and lost
> oxygen (an ecological site calculated that newsprint production used up the
> equivalent of 453 million trees in 2001); no more gas-sucking, pollution-spewing
> trucks to haul them around; no more presses draining energy; no more waste to
> recycle; no more oil pumped to make ink. To hell with going carbon-neutral. A
> former paper is an ecological hero!   (Jarvis, 2009)

A world where news publishers no longer rely on paper as the primary
medium for delivering their content may not be too far away. Jarvis (2009)
recounts a talk given in 2005 by Alan Rusbridger, editor of the *Guardian* in
the UK, where he stated the paper's newly installed printing presses would
probably be the last they would ever buy.

However, despite the lower costs involved in producing online news there
are also fewer opportunities for publishers to generate income. Most printed
newspapers still charge a cover price to readers, which makes a substantial
contribution to the overall revenue of the publisher. In Japan and much of
Europe, cover prices contribute over 50% to total newspaper revenues, with
advertising making up the rest (OECD, 2010). Most US newspapers operate
on a different revenue model with copy prices only averaging 13% of total
revenues. While many people, albeit a declining number, are still prepared
to pay for a printed newspaper there is less willingness to do the same for
online news. Many online news sites have chosen to follow an advertising-

based revenue model reflecting both the lower costs in news delivery as shown in Figure 2.2 and the abundance of news-related information that exists on the internet. Whereas printed papers are a limited resource for all the reasons that characterize physical media, a news website is only a click away, resulting in a commodification of news and, it could be argued, a devaluing of this type of content.

The transition to digital news

Research from the World Association of Newspapers and News Publishers (WAN-IFRA), which represents news publishers globally, shows that in the five years leading up to 2014 there was a significant drop in print sales of newspapers in developed economies but a rise in developing countries (WAN-IFRA, 2014). WAN-IFRA claims this is due to the growing middle classes in emerging economies, which drives demand for news and comment. While printed newspaper sales fall in the developed world and digital news consumption increases, the ability of digital content to generate sufficient revenues for publishers is in doubt. According to WAN-IFRA Secretary General Larry Kilman, this is a concern for news groups but also for society more generally: 'Unless we crack the revenue issue, and provide sufficient funds so that newspapers can fulfil their societal role, democracy will inevitably be weakened' (WAN-IFRA, 2014).

Addressing Kilman's and most of the established news publishing industry's concerns about revenue loss requires online publishers to either adopt a subscription-based business model and/or generate income from advertising. Selling advertising space on news websites was the preferred model for most publishers, but many of them found this was not sufficient to make up for the lost income from paper copy sales. The *MailOnline* in the UK shows signs of being an exception to this rule. Its combination of gossip and celebrity news has made it one of the most visited 'news' sites in the world. In July 2014 it claimed to have over 56 million monthly unique visitors globally (MailOnline, 2014) and, according to Sweney (2014), by early 2014 was generating almost £5 million a month from advertising sales. Some more specialist news providers, mainly those offering financial news, such as the *Financial Times* in the UK and the *Wall Street Journal* in the USA, have managed to operate successful paywalls for their online content. The stories, commentary and analysis they offer is attractive to an audience with deeper pockets than most general news consumers although more general news publishers have had some success with their own paywalls. Since 2010, the UK-based publishers of *The Times*, *Sunday Times* and *Telegraph* have introduced paywalls and subscription packages for online access to much of their content. Despite many predictions that these moves would generate very few paying subscribers, the evidence is that there may be a future for this type of news delivery. The New York Times is one of the most successful publishers to try the subscription model, and according to Beaujon (2014) had over 760,000 paying subscribers by the end of 2013.

However, despite the relatively promising developments for established news groups presented above the industry is still in the throes of a painful transition. How many print-based titles will be able to make a successful transition to a digital-only world remains to be seen. Even the online success of the *New York Times* is no guarantee that it will be able to compete commercially with a range of new entrants coming into the market. A leaked internal review by the *New York Times* has highlighted the challenges to established publishers presented by new entrants to the market (Benton, 2014). The review presents a frank and considered appraisal of these challenges and argues that a new mindset is needed by newspaper publishers if they are to compete successfully with digital-only companies such as the Huffington Post, Business Insider and BuzzFeed (see case study on page 27). The review's authors claim that these are the main threats to the *New York Times*, not other papers such as the *Washington Post*. The report suggests that one way of doing this is to remove the traditional separation of the editorial and the business sides of the business and make journalists more commercially aware of what types of content are popular. This needs to be managed very carefully if publishers are to maintain ethical standards over the separation of editorial and advertising.

Digital-only news publishers

Where do blogs and other online-only publishers fit into the news ecosystem and what impacts are they having on the print media? Despite predictions to the contrary, news blogs have not replaced traditional news providers and are unlikely to do so in the near to medium term. However, they are having an impact particularly in the area of specialist news normally provided by so-called 'trade publishers'. In the USA, perhaps the most widely viewed and well known mainstream online news site is the Huffington Post, which offers its readers news and comment with a liberal leaning. The most popular of the Australian independent general news blogs is Crikey.com.au, which offers a website and subscription-based e-mail service. In November 2012, Crikey claimed it delivered over 2.1 million page impressions to 398,000 unique visitors, which compares reasonably favourably to Australia's highest circulation print newspaper, the *Sunday Telegraph*, which had a circulation of 600,236 in September 2012 (AdNews, 2012). While some news websites are attracting large audiences it is not clear to what extent they are contributing to the decline of print sales, which have been decreasing for several decades (OECD, 2010).

Other factors, including the popularity of television news and changing lifestyles, may also be significant. While there is no home-grown equivalent to Crikey or the Huffington Post in the UK, a number of newspapers have been keen adopters of blogs to extend their reach across the internet. All British newspapers have their own websites where stories and commentary from their print editions are reproduced, and a number of them also give their journalists blogs, which are embedded in the main news site. Blogging allows the print journalists to respond quickly to news stories and publish material that did not make it into print editions for space or editorial reasons. From the publisher's perspective this is an extremely cost-effective way of producing more content for their readers. Free from the restraints of print and paper, the reproduction costs of digital information is marginal. In July 2014, the Guardian website was hosting 62 blogs on subjects from technology, media and the environment to music, film, politics and gardening. The Guardian bike blog, for example, has a core team of five bloggers plus other occasional contributors. Posts are added every couple of days but it is the interaction with readers that generates the most information. Depending on the subject being discussed there are varying levels of debate and discussion among commentators but 80 or more comments on a single post is not unusual. By focusing on a niche subject such as cycling, a following of committed readers can be developed which allows publishers such as the Guardian to develop deeper relationships with its readers than is possible with printed papers.

Although a mainstream newspaper and a lone blogger may use the same platform to publish their writing to the internet, a key difference between them is that writers for newspapers are usually professional journalists while the lone blogger is often not. This does not necessarily mean the blogger's outputs are inferior, but for some people at least they need to be seen in this context. Luckhurst, himself a former newspaper editor, feels strongly that amateur bloggers are not in the same league as their professional counterparts: 'The essential difference between the two deserves definition. It is that much blogging is an amateur activity carried out by people with no understanding of journalism's social purpose who operate with scant regard for facts' (Luckhurst, 2011).

Luckhurst may have a valid point if one is comparing a newspaper directly with a blog but perhaps this comparison is unfair. It might be argued that blogs should be seen as supplementary to the outputs of traditional news publishers and not as replacements. In this respect they are similar to podcasts; mainstream radio broadcasters still produce programmes but amateur podcasters have stepped in to fill some of the gaps for niche audiences.

The new generation of news consumers

The popularity of smart phones across developed economies since 2010, particularly among younger consumers, is creating a new audience for news providers among people who were not traditionally large purchasers of newspapers. Established news publishers have optimized their websites to be more readable on smaller phone and tablet screens, and in many instances have created dedicated applications to deliver their content. New entrants to this market have capitalized on this development and created news sites that are optimized for all screen sizes, publish content that is easily shareable across social media, and know how to create headlines that will appeal to a younger, internet-savvy generation. News industry analyst Ken Doctor estimates that the barriers to entry for new digital-only publishers is low with only US$5 million to US$10 million needed per year to run an operation comprising 20 journalists (Gapper, 2014). Although this might sound like a large sum, it is tiny compared with the costs of setting up a print-based news business. Marc Andreessen, founder of Netscape and a partner in one of the leading US venture capital firms, sees massive opportunities for the news sector with new jobs being created as traditional printing presses are shut down: 'I am more bullish about the future of the news industry over the next 20 years than almost anyone I know. You are going to see it grow 10X to 100X from where it is today. . . . Maybe we are entering into a new golden age of journalism, and we just haven't recognized it yet' (Andreessen, 2014).

As an investor in news startups, Andreessen obviously has a vested interest in promoting their growth but more objective evidence supporting his predictions can be seen from the respected Pew Research Center in the USA. Their annual research into the evolving news sector shows that in the USA in the ten years to 2014 almost 500 new companies were set up employing approximately 5000 full-time journalists (Jurkowitz, 2014). While this figure is lower than that of the number of jobs lost in traditional news companies over the same period, it offers hope that the industry will be commercially sustainable in the future. In the same way that printed papers range from quality titles such as the *Financial Times* and the *New York Times* to less serious papers like the *Sun* and the *National Enquirer*, so too do the digital news sites. At the serious end are sites including The Intercept and Five Thirty Eight, in the middle Vox and at the more popular end BuzzFeed. A key factor in the success of these new sites is the ease with which their content is shared across social media platforms and onto mobile devices, making them increasingly important sources of news for younger audiences (Mitchell et al, 2013).

CASE STUDY BuzzFeed

BuzzFeed was founded in New York in 2006 and describes itself as a 'social news and entertainment company'; it claims a global audience of over 130 million internet users. Principally known for creating viral content that encourages sharing across the internet via social media, the company has been accused by some critics of plagiarizing stories and content from other sites without attribution. However, its diet of videos and stories such as 'Did you know penguins have knees?' and '19 things that happen when you date a scientist' have made it one of the most popular news sites on the internet. By mid-2014 the company employed more than 300 people and, through a focus on sponsored content rather than relying solely on advertising, is profitable. This is not something that can be said of many traditional news publishers. A key factor in BuzzFeed's success is its sophisticated use of analytics to track the consumption of its content and to feed this back into the editorial process to optimize consumer interest. Although seen as a threat to major news organizations by some industry observers others question whether a diet of animated cat gifs and a focus on trivia will allow the company to evolve into a more serious entity.

Business publishing

As mainstream news tries to adapt to the low-cost, online publishing revolution, specialist news and information providers are arguably feeling the pressure more. This is particularly true with business to business (B2B) publishers, which produce information resources aimed at professionals working in the public and private sectors. These publications cater to very specific needs of information technology (IT), software buyers and people managing logistics functions such as shipping and road haulage and other sectors. The titles of some of the publications in the B2B arena point to these specialisms, for example, *Solicitors Journal, Pipeline and Gas Journal, Retail Week, Container Management* and *Floor Covering Weekly*. B2B publishers vary from very small operations that may produce only one or two very niche titles to large groups such as EMAP, Wolters Kluwer and Springer in Europe, and Hearst Business Media and Penton Media in the USA.

Traditionally, B2B publishing has been highly profitable as publishers have been able to deliver to highly targeted audiences that often have high spending power to advertisers. If you are a producer of flooring products in the USA then *Floor Covering Weekly* is a key channel for reaching flooring contractors and distributors who make up the bulk of readers of this publication. Many B2B publishers offer free subscriptions to qualified readers because the profit is in selling the advertising. However, as many business professionals move away from relying on specialist magazines as a source of information to using the internet, B2B publishing has become a lot less profitable for many companies. One of the reasons for this move away from print media is the opportunity that blogs and other websites allow industry experts to develop their own platforms for knowledge sharing and bypass the publishers. As a consequence and perhaps as a demonstration of a lack of confidence in the future of traditional B2B publishing a number of publishers including VNU, The Nielsen Company and Reed Elsevier have sold off their magazine businesses.

Research in Europe and the USA by PricewaterhouseCoopers highlights the challenges posed by the electronic delivery of information. In a survey, many business professionals expressed a preference to obtain their information online. Similarly Fenez and van der Donk (2010) found that 60% of those surveyed visit a business website at least once a week. Although the PricewaterhouseCoopers research shows there is still demand for printed publications, the large B2B publishers now generate almost half their revenues through online activities. Fenez and van der Donk see a long-term overall decline in the global advertising revenues of B2B publishers but believe that online advertising will increase as a proportion of the total at the expense of print advertising. The future, they argue, lies in publishers exploiting their valuable content and embedding their information services via live feeds and dynamic content into the work flows of their customers in a more active way than simply publishing magazines: 'The industry has moved on from simply being an aggregator of business-specific news. The priority now is to take advantage of all channels to become established as a trusted source of informed content. To do this and maintain their relevance, B2B publishers should be leveraging social networking trends' (Fenez and van der Donk, 2010, 5).

A number of specialist publishers are starting to follow this advice by broadening their information portfolios and using the internet to integrate their content into organizations' processes and workflows in ways that were not possible with paper publications. In 2013 Elsevier, one of the world's largest publishers of medical and scientific titles, purchased the engineering information company Knovel, which describes itself as a 'cloud-based application integrating technical information with analytical and search tools to drive innovation and deliver answers engineers can trust'. Essentially, Knovel aggregates engineering data from hundreds of respected publications and allows engineers to search across that content and input their own data into equations in an interactive format, which is compatible with commonly used software such as Excel. This allows engineers to integrate valuable third party information into their own projects in an efficient and streamlined way. The purchase of Knovel enables Elsevier's intellectual property to move from dusty shelves in university and corporate libraries straight to the computers of its end-users.

Failing to adapt to the social web could become an increasing problem for B2B publishers as they find themselves squeezed between large and established social networks such as LinkedIn and Facebook and smaller, niche blogs and online communities, which have no legacy print operations that impose cost burdens and restrict profitability. Whether this will lead to a transforming state of 'creative destruction' as described by Schumpeter (1950), whereby a new technology or set of technologies supplant an established way of doing business, remains to be seen. However, it is already the case that many print-centric B2B publishers that have not developed their web presence are becoming less relevant to their core audiences. David Gilbertson, chief executive of publisher EMAP, describes how his business is responding to the digital challenge: 'The way I'd describe [the shift] is moving from the provision of information to providing intelligence. Companies like ourselves need to suggest what decision should arise, rather than just record that something occurred' (Bintliff, 2011).

Across a number of business sectors, web-based publishers such as Freepint, Sift and GigaOm (see case study below) are becoming trusted sources of information for professionals while social media sites such as LinkedIn allow like-minded professionals from all industries to form loose associations. LinkedIn groups allow any LinkedIn member to create an online discussion group around a specific area of interest. By July 2014, LinkedIn hosted more than 2.1 million groups based around commercial areas such as telecommunications, advertising and human resources to non-profit and alumni interest groups. Membership ranges from over 900,000 members for the Human Resources Group down to lower numbers for more niche interests. These groups can be seen as shared blogs where questions are posted, answers given, polls run and opinions shared. Although there is a concern that some groups are dominated by members trying to sell their services to other members, many offer vibrant online communities. They and the plethora of special-interest blogs that exist outside LinkedIn offer a new, more democratic channel for professionals to communicate and share information than was ever possible when traditional publishers dominated.

Many of the large B2B publishers are aware of the increasing preference for online information delivery among their professional readers and have been active in developing online spaces to distribute their content, for example Knovel and Elsevier described above. Perhaps indicative of the longer-term analogue future of B2B magazine publishing, in December 2013 Lloyds List ceased producing paper versions of its shipping industry publication. This may not seem a particularly momentous occasion except that it was the oldest printed business publication dating back to 1734. According to Greenslade (2013) the publication is still the key source for its sector but research carried out by its owner, Informa, showed that 97% preferred to read Lloyds List content online with only 2% reading the paper copy.

CASE STUDY GigaOm

GigaOm is a website built on the WordPress blogging platform founded in 2006 by Om Malik, a US-based technology analyst, and offering expert commentary and analysis on a range of technology sectors. In July 2014 it was claiming over 6.5 million unique monthly visitors. Using a range of contributors, GigaOm claims it 'is committed to bringing solid journalism to the web with a strategy that is grounded in the belief that media sites are no longer just publications, but rather hubs of business communities'. While the blog is free for anyone to access, GigaOm also offers a premium service allowing paying subscribers to access more detailed research and reports the company produces, accessible in a variety of digital formats such as PDF and HTML. GigaOm is not as large as more traditional publishers in this sector, such as Forrester or Gartner, but its US$299 annual individual subscription cost is considerably less and presents an attractive alternative for small companies not able to afford the many thousands of dollars that larger competitors charge for similar information.

Wikis and collaborative publishing

The previous section showed some of the challenges facing traditional news and specialist publishers from the rise of new online sources of information, in particular blogs. While online publishing presents a definite challenge and opportunity to print publishers, it can be seen as an evolutionary development in information production, as commercially driven sites still require a formal editorial process and need to generate revenues from advertising or subscriptions. Allied to this is the necessity for the people producing the content to be paid in some form or other. This section will consider another electronic challenge to print publishers in the form of the wiki as a publishing platform. Although wikis are more typically used as online collaborative platforms to share information within and across groups, the success of Wikipedia presents a revolutionary development in information production.

From a technical perspective, wikis differ from blogs in that they are a much more flexible platform for allowing users to add and edit content posted to the wiki site. In its most basic form, a wiki can be seen as a blank canvas on which users, depending on the permissions they have been given, can create pages and add text, links, images and other content. Another crucial feature of a wiki is that existing content can be edited and even removed by users. Where successfully deployed a wiki is a dynamic online space that reflects the needs and interests of its contributors without the constraints imposed by more structured content management systems such as blogs. Although this flexibility may be seen as a strength of wikis, it could also be viewed as a weakness. The formal structure of a blog results in information being presented in a generally consistent manner that can be easily understood by its readers, and in theory at least, a wiki could be an anarchic collection of disparate and disorganized content. Wikipedia demonstrates this need not be the case and shows how many thousands of contributors spread across the globe can create a trusted and valuable reference source for millions of internet users.

Wikipedia was created in the USA in 2001 by entrepreneur Jimmy Wales and philosopher Larry Sanger. In July 2014 it comprised over 32.5 million articles (1600 times as many as Encyclopaedia Britannica), is available in 287 languages and attracts over 500 million visitors a month, making it the world's sixth most popular website (Wikipedia, 2013). As part of the Wikimedia Foundation, in 2014, Wikipedia is sustained by approximately 140 employees. Being able to maintain the creation of this much content along with the 12 million monthly edits that take place within Wikipedia would be impossible with this level of resources if it were not for the unpaid contributors who produce the information. While there is a relatively small core of unpaid 'Wikipedians' who oversee the production and editing of much of the site's content, most of the entries are open for any internet user to edit. Creating new pages is almost as easy as editing them, but requires registration first, a free and straightforward process. With so few barriers preventing users from adding nonsensical or inaccurate information or from defacing the work of others it is perhaps not surprising that many commentators and educators were initially very sceptical about the veracity of Wikipedia and its value as a trusted reference source. Many schools and universities still prohibit students from citing Wikipedia in their work, although this seems to be changing as its value becomes recognized.

A number of tests have been carried out to compare the accuracy of Wikipedia with more established reference sources. Perhaps the most famous was in 2005 when the Nature Publishing Group compared a number of science-based entries between Wikipedia and Encyclopaedia Britannica and found little to choose between them in degree of accuracy. Although Encyclopaedia Britannica disputed the findings it was a watershed moment for Wikipedia and forced a number of sceptics to take a second look. Wikipedia would claim that what a number of critics see as its primary weakness is actually one of its key strengths: while almost anyone may add data to the site, the same people may also amend, edit and delete information they see as inaccurate or too trivial for inclusion. Working on the assumption that the number of people who care about creating and curating a valuable information resource outnumber those who would like to deface and undermine it, Wikipedia provides evidence of the power of collaboration.

Whatever the motives of those who contribute to this global experiment in information production, it is not financial and that could present a serious challenge to the business models of commercial publishers, especially established publishers of encyclopedias. Encyclopaedia Britannica has been struggling since the early 1990s when competitors, particularly Encarta, started to offer encyclopedias on CD-ROM. As personal computers started to appear in homes and on desktops these digital versions were particularly attractive as they were easier to navigate, much cheaper, able to deliver multimedia and did not require the shelf space needed for the 32 Britannica volumes. Not surprisingly, Britannica went online a number of years ago but has adopted a subscription model making it far less attractive to the mass of internet users who have grown up expecting information to be free and instantly accessible. Even Microsoft's Encarta encyclopedia on CD-ROM, Britannica's first digital challenger, gave in to the challenge of Wikipedia and closed down in 2009 after 16 years of production. In 2012 Britannica announced that it would no longer publish printed copies of its encyclopedias, marking the end of an almost 250 year tradition and offering further evidence of the difficulties for analogue information producers in a digital and networked world.

However, the future for Wikipedia is not certain. Although it is the single most popular source of reference information on the web and has proven that its volunteer model can work to produce generally accurate and valued information, it still requires income to operate. As the site carries no advertising and has no subscription model its revenues have been largely from donations. In 2013 it raised over US$50 million in donations and grants, which has secured the finances of the Wikimedia Foundation for the immediate future, but concerns have been raised over whether the volunteer model is sustainable over the next decade. According to Simonite (2014), this volunteer workforce has shrunk by more than one-third since 2007. A result of this and the 90% dominance of male writers largely from developed economies is that Wikipedia entries tend to be skewed to subjects of most interest to such a demographic. Simonite points out, 'Its entries on Pokemon and female porn stars are comprehensive, but its pages on female novelists or places in sub-Saharan Africa are sketchy' (Simonite, 2014, 52).

Efforts are under way by the Wikimedia Foundation to try and rectify this imbalance but as volunteers are not paid it is difficult to enforce change on people who cannot be made to conform as in a normal organization.

Perhaps a sign that Wikipedia is gaining respectability, or at least acceptance, within the 'establishment' was a recent joint endeavour between the online encyclopedia and the British Museum. The museum allowed a Wikipedia contributor and expert on antiquities to spend five weeks in the institution to help museum staff understand how Wikipedia works and show them how they can edit and improve content on the site. Acknowledging that Wikipedia is a starting point for many online researchers, the British Museum's head of web explained the initiative: 'If we are going to accept that many people are going to use it to read about our objects [on Wikipedia], why not collaborate and make that article on Wikipedia as good as we can get it by working with them' (Hitchcock, 2011).

Search engines and what they know

While search engines such as Google and Bing are the primary tools most people use when finding information on the internet they also generate vast amounts of information in their own right. According to *The Economist* (2010), every time we use a search engine and then click through the pages it provides we leave a trail of 'data exhaust' behind us providing a rich source of information for marketers, academics and anyone else interested in human behaviour. Battelle (2006) points out that the search giant Google is compiling a global 'database of intentions' built from the enquiries millions of us type into its search box every day. Before the mass adoption of the internet as an information resource, an understanding of the information needs and wishes of end-users was primarily confined to reference librarians. They were the focal point for enquiries by library patrons who could not locate the information they required by themselves. Although directories, encyclopedias and other reference sources were widely consulted by information seekers, the producers of these resources had no idea of the actual needs of those using them. Thousands of patrons may look for information in a library's directory of local businesses but their enquiries leave no trace once the directory has been closed and returned to the shelves. In contrast, an internet search engine maintains a log of the words people enter into the search box, allowing patterns of search behaviour to be observed and a deeper understanding of what people are most interested in.

Although there are a number of internet search engines freely available, Google is the dominant global player. Its market share varies between countries, from approximately 90% in the UK, to 60% in the USA and 20% in China. Although Google has extended its business into a number of other areas including mobile phones, ownership of YouTube, ebooks and e-mail,

91% of its annual revenue in 2013 came from providing a platform for online advertising. By understanding from their search requests what it is that people are interested in, Google was able to generate US$50.5 billion in 2013 from placing relevant advertisements next to its search results and relevant content on other websites. According to Google's own figures, in 2012 the company was handling approximately 38,000 search queries per second, equivalent to 3.3 billion searches per day (Sullivan, 2012b). This equates to more than 1.2 trillion searches a year, giving Google a unique insight into what is on the minds of the more than 1 billion people around the world who use the service regularly.

While Google has been able to put this information to extremely profitable use with its AdWords programme, which places relevant online advertisements next to search results, third parties are also mining this new source of information for the insights it contains. Using the free online service Google Trends, anyone can compare the frequency with which specific words and phrases are entered into the Google search box and then analyse how this varies over time and between geographic regions. This can be useful for marketing professionals as it allows comparisons of search activity between theirs and competing products. A comparison of 'coke' and 'pepsi' as search terms performed in July 2014 revealed, perhaps not surprisingly, 'coke' to be a moderately more popular search term than 'pepsi'. However, drilling down into the data showed that in some countries such as Guatemala there were far more searches for 'pepsi' than 'coke'. This might be because of specific marketing activity for one or both those brands focused on that country and would certainly be of interest to management at the companies. Although this is a fairly trivial example it indicates the value that this 'data exhaust' has. Companies that sell products or services via their websites use this data to make sure they are including appropriate words on their sites. One of the variables that Google and other search engines take into account when presenting search results is how closely the words used on a website match the search terms a user has entered. For example, if you sell mobile phones through your website, knowing the most popular words and phrases related to mobile phones that people are entering into Google allows you to optimize the text on the pages you want people to visit.

Gaming Google

In the previous section we saw how website owners can use tools such as Google Trends to optimize the text-based content on their sites to match more closely the words and phrases that users type into search engines when searching for information on specific topics. When Google indexes a web page it analyses the keywords it contains, where they appear on the page and their frequency to determine what the page is about. This data is then stored in its index and it is this index we search against when using the search engine. If you manage a website and want to be indexed correctly by Google and other search engines it is therefore important to understand how this process works, and to realize that keywords are only one signal which search engines take into account when deciding which web pages to show in search results. One of the key signals behind Google's search algorithm and which determines ranking in search results is the number and quality of links from other pages to a specific page. We can be certain that many web pages have been optimized for the search term 'Florida holidays', but how does Google decide which of the many hundreds in its index it should put on the first page of search results when someone types the phrase into its search box? This is where the significance of incoming links from other pages becomes apparent. A web page that has the phrase 'Florida holidays' in all the right places but which no other web page has linked to will rank lower in the order of results than one which may look similar but has links from other reputable sites. Search engines interpret these links as votes of confidence in the quality of a web page in a similar way that academic research is often judged by the citations it has received in other academic publications.

Since the late 1990s a new sub-sector of the marketing industry has emerged known as search engine optimization. Practitioners of search engine optimization seek to integrate best practice in the optimization of web pages so that they rank as highly as possible in search results. While this is a logical development in a world where commercial websites need to be found in search results, it has also spawned a new type of web content from organizations often referred to as 'content farms'. These are a product of the success of Google as a search engine and its success as an advertising platform. Google's AdSense program allows any website owner to host Google's AdWords advertisements on its pages. Whenever anyone clicks on those advertisements, the website owner receives a percentage of the revenue generated. This extends the locations where Google can place its advertisements beyond just search results pages, and offers website owners a revenue stream and an opportunity to monetize their content. This opportunity has encouraged the growth of content farms and other producers of often low-quality content, which seek to rank highly in search results and make a profit from the advertisements they run alongside this content. The articles published by these companies are typically written by freelancers who may be paid only several dollars for each one. It has been estimated than one of the largest content farms, Demand Media, was publishing over 4000 articles and videos a day at its peak in 2009 (Roth, 2009).

This new model of information production was unprecedented in the history of the publishing industry in its prolific output and its rapid rise. However, an industry based on the mass production of low-cost and often low-quality information is probably not sustainable. Companies such as Demand Media have been very successful in producing web-based content which ranks highly in search engine results, but they have not always been popular with search engine companies such as Google or their users. From a user perspective, a search engine is only as good as the quality and relevance of the results it returns. Although content farms may produce content that meets the relevance threshold, they often do not match a user's quality expectations. Google's fear that its users will switch to a different search engine such as Bing because of poor quality results has been a growing concern. As a consequence, it has made a series of significant changes to the ways it ranks the authority of the pages it indexes, which has had a detrimental effect on the companies producing what it sees as low-quality information. The first of these major changes was known as the Panda algorithm, which was implemented in February 2011, followed by other adjustments: Penguin in 2012 and Hummingbird in 2013. The impact on the content farms was dramatic as their positions in search engine results fell and their visitor numbers dropped as a result. In the months following the Panda update, for example, the share price of Demand Media fell by almost 75% and three years later had still not recovered, according to data from the Google Finance website.

In some respects, Google can be seen as a victim of its own success. By becoming the dominant portal through which many internet users start their information seeking journey, it has created a platform for new types of information producers to flourish. Where these producers offer high-quality and relevant content, Google's offering is enhanced. However, when these producers learn how to get round the criteria by which Google presents information to its users then the reputation of the search engine suffers. As long as search engines provide the primary starting point for information retrieval requests then this struggle to filter out those seeking to game the algorithm will continue.

Does Google know too much?

The value of our search data to Google is obvious in that it has resulted in a 16-year-old company founded by two university students being valued at US$408 billion by the stock market. We have seen earlier that this data is also of value to marketers as they try to understand what people are interested in and how to tailor their messages to match that interest. However, there are growing concerns that Google is becoming too powerful and that the data it holds on its users' search behaviour and the web pages it has indexed have created a company with unprecedented control over and access to personal data on a global scale. In 2012 Google revealed that it was able to identify more than 30 trillion unique uniform resource locators (URLs) or individual web pages and that its automated search bot was crawling and indexing 20 billion sites a day (Sullivan, 2012b). Instant and free access to search this massive index allows us to find references to others on long-forgotten web pages at the press of a button. For serious research purposes this is of immense value but from a personal privacy perspective it presents a number of challenges. Should anyone have access to a photo of us drunk at a party taken when we were a student 20 years previously and which still sits on a forgotten web page? Should a local news report of a shoplifting incident from 15 years ago still be accessible via Google when the person concerned is now a responsible parent?

Following concerns in Europe that Google's index of web pages was violating individuals' rights to privacy, in May 2014 EU regulators ruled that links to 'irrelevant' and out-of-date information should be removed from search results when requested. Known as a 'right to be forgotten', the ruling has been controversial not just within Google but also among critics who claim it is an attack on the right to free speech. The 2014 ruling does not require that any web pages be removed from the web but that Google and other search engines not provide links to them in search results when a specific name is entered in the search box. Major search engines operating in Europe have provided forms which individuals can fill in by inputting their name and the URLs of pages they want removing from results. In the three months after May 2014, Google claimed it had received 90,000 requests relating to 300,000 web pages and had approved more than half of these requests (Mason, 2014). Although welcomed by many personal privacy campaigners, this development has raised concerns by those concerned that Google's willingness to remove content from its search results is restricting free speech on the part of publishers and may also allow those with criminal pasts to evade investigations that are in the public interest.

One of the unintended consequences of this ruling is that those requesting the removal of links may actually find themselves in the public eye more prominently than before they submitted the request. The Irish data protection commissioner is concerned that as media organizations are notified by Google that some of their pages have been removed from search results, they are simply republishing the original stories and as a consequence reminding readers about individuals who had probably been forgotten (White, 2014). It is too early to understand fully what the implications for information retrieval and research practices are of this ruling but it perhaps presages a push-back by the state and citizens against the rapid growth of corporations such as Google and Facebook.

Our social graphs

Google's 'database of intentions' may have its finger on the pulse of what internet users are interested in but for the most part this data is fairly anonymous. One of the key technologies driving the so-called Web 2.0 revolution was social networking, which allowed us to forge virtual links with others online. MySpace and Friendster were two of the original social networking services but both have since been eclipsed by Facebook, which in June 2014 claimed to have more than 1.3 billion active users, almost half of all global users of the internet. Other social networks of note are the micro-blogging service Twitter and LinkedIn, which focuses on professional credentials, providing networking opportunities and a form of online CV. Like Google, they provide services that users value and they generate rich and valuable data for their owners about who is connected to who, what they are saying to each other and, through the groups they belong to and links they share, what their interests are. Facebook has copied Google to the extent that it presents advertisements which it considers will be of interest to its users, but the method it uses to target these advertisements differs in that it draws on what it knows about its users. This information comes from the data we give Facebook about our age, gender, location, marital status, education and personal interests when we open an account. Advertisers are then able to construct advertising campaigns, which they present only to specific types of people. In itself this is a new source of information to the extent that no single organization has held this much data on the personal characteristics of so many people. The direct marketing industry has long made use of such data to help target their direct mail campaigns but it has had to rely on datasets of personal information from a range of providers, much of it out of date and inaccurate, or based on generalized assumptions about the areas people live in. Facebook's database is far more dynamic, and is updated in almost real time by its users either directly or by their actions. For example, change your Facebook profile from married to single and you will probably start to see advertisements for dating agencies appearing on your pages. Change again from single to engaged and companies offering photographic services and other wedding-related offerings will appear.

This chapter is concerned with new models of information production and it could be argued that what Facebook has created is just a more sophisticated and larger database of personal information than has existed before. If this were all it had done then that might be a fair criticism. However, it is the addition of the social layer of information on top of this personal data that makes it unique. Knowing that Sarah is single, 31 years old, university educated and works as a nurse in the George Washington University Hospital in Washington DC is valuable information to the many companies and organizations that would like to communicate with her for commercial and non-commercial reasons. However, knowing this and who her friends are, what they talk about online, the Facebook groups she belongs to, web pages she 'likes', photos she has uploaded and events she has attended starts to build a complex and detailed picture of her. Extend this level of detail across the 1.3 billion plus users of Facebook and the argument that this is a new model of information production seems reasonable. In this instance we, as users, are a primary source of information creation. This is a virtuous circle of content being created for free by Facebook's users, which because of its personal nature is of interest to friends and family of those users.

Companies have been quick to recognize the potential of this platform to promote their goods and services by creating pages and content which they hope users will 'like', resulting in the company's future content appearing in users' news feeds. Those companies able to create appealing and shareable content are rewarded with a large and targetable audience without having to pay Facebook for the privilege. However, the success of Facebook has also presented it a challenge similar to Google's described earlier. According to Wagner (2013), the average Facebook user has 1500 new items which could appear in their news feed every day, forcing Facebook to develop an algorithm which will decide which items to actually show. Presenting all 1500 items would be overwhelming and so priority has to be given to those likely to be of most interest. It is likely that a post from a user's relative or friend will be more relevant and interesting than a post from a company which the user 'liked' three years previously. While users may benefit by seeing the content they want, companies have lost out as nearly all their unpaid for content is now never seen. This has driven revenues for Facebook as sponsored content has become the only guaranteed way to appear in news feeds. This may seem a trivial matter to anyone not trying to promote their company's products or services over this network, but it has a broader significance for the evolution of the internet and the world wide web. As we increasingly suffer from information overload as friends, family and companies vie for our attention online, tools that allow us to filter the important from the trivial will become more important. A key question is whether corporate interests can be aligned with users' interests in the design of these solutions. Companies like Facebook and Twitter need to tread a careful line if they are not to turn the social web into just another channel for advertising and commercial activities.

Apart from being able to help deliver more targeted advertisements to Facebook users, what is this data being used for? At the moment marketing is the main focus of commercial activity but a number of other applications are becoming apparent. Rosenbloom (2007) describes the value that this data has for social scientists interested in mapping and measuring how people communicate and interact online. She quotes Harvard sociology professor Nicholas Christakis on the potential of social media platforms for academic research: 'We're on the cusp of a new way of doing social science. Our predecessors could only dream of the kind of data we now have' (Rosenbloom, 2007). Christakis was this enthusiastic when Facebook only had 58 million active users; with more than 20 times this number using the network in mid-2014, the value to social scientists can only have increased. This is evidenced by research such as Claussen, Kretschmer and Mayrhofer's (2013) study into motivation and user engagement on social media and Fuchs et al.'s (2012) collection of research into state and corporate surveillance and social media. When a service like Facebook becomes so ubiquitous, it can almost be seen as a utility like water or the telephone network, which we take for granted and use unconsciously as part of our everyday lives. In this scenario it is possible to imagine it being used as a barometer for governments to gauge the mood of their citizens, a channel for important messages such as severe weather warnings to be distributed, or just a place to locate and communicate with like-minded people.

As well as these benign uses for Facebook's rapidly growing database, there is the obvious and much discussed issue of privacy. Do we trust a company set up by a college student in 2004 with the often deeply personal data of hundreds of millions of people? Many do not and we will explore the privacy aspects of social networking later in this book. The revelation that in 2012 Facebook experimented on 700,000 of its users by trying to affect their moods through content filtering without asking for permission is perhaps an indication that we need to be alert (BBC, 2014).

What are we worth?

As social media services become more commercial to satisfy the demands of their shareholders, users become the sources of value that, in the jargon of the financial markets, need to be monetized. This is no different from ways that traditional print and broadcast media have approached their businesses for decades. However, a key difference is that as viewers and readers we have long understood this pact: newspapers, magazines and television broadcasters will invest their own money to create content which we are happy to consume and pay for through subscriptions and/or being exposed to advertisements. In a social media world where we are both the producers and the consumers of information, this willingness to accept advertisements may not be of concern for many users but there is an emerging school of thought which believes we are giving away more value to companies such as Facebook than we are receiving. Aligned to this is the oft quoted saying,

'If you're not paying for the service then you're not the customer, you're the product.'

Lanier (2013) has taken this concern further and argues that creators of web content should be compensated for their efforts by receiving micro-payments when it is consumed by others. It is unlikely that such a system could ever be successfully implemented, at least under the current underlying infrastructure of the world wide web, but there are commercial initiatives which seek to compensate web users for the marketing value of their personal data. US-based company Datacoup offers anyone who signs up for its service US$8 a month for access to their Facebook, Twitter and financial data, which it then sells on to data brokers and other third parties who use it for marketing purposes. Klout, another US company (see case study below), does not offer its users any financial compensation but gives them scores based on their online activity and popularity on social networks. While initiatives such as Datacoup and Klout may raise a number of ethical and privacy issues, they perhaps point the way to a world where consumers may be able to take more control over the data they generate during their daily activities. Whether individuals make use of such tools will, like many online services, depend on levels of awareness and education and will feed into ongoing debates over information literacy and digital divides.

CASE STUDY KLOUT

Klout was established in 2008 and offers its users the chance to monitor their social media 'influence'. It claims to take over 400 data points from eight different social networks including Facebook and Twitter and measures more than 1.2 billion signals every day. Although every Twitter user who has not opted out of the Klout service is automatically given a social influence score, registered users are able to integrate the other seven social networks to create a broader based total score. In some senses Klout is a natural evolution of the popularity of social networking services and the need for marketers to identify influencers. Klout's business model is based on making deals with companies wishing to offer 'perks' to its users, which normally involves special offers and free products and services. In 2013, American Airlines announced that any air travellers with a Klout score above 55 would be given free access to their executive lounges at 40 airports around the world. However, some critics do not see Klout as a benign service for social media enthusiasts but rather as an attempt to put a value on our social relationships and playing to the narcissistic tendencies of some internet users. There have been reports of job seekers not being shortlisted for interview because their Klout scores were deemed too low. Whatever the pros and cons of Klout, in early 2014 the company was bought for a reported US$200 million by Lithium

Technologies, indicating that a value can be attached to knowing about our online social relationships.

So far this chapter has shown how internet-based services such as social media and online searching are producing new types of information that are being used by marketers to better understand our needs and desires. We have also seen how low-cost, easy to use self-publishing platforms such as blogs and wikis are impacting on more traditional publishers. The next section explores the emerging world of big data and the 'internet of things' where the physical world of new technologies are throwing out information in quantities presenting new challenges for information management professionals.

The challenge of big data

So far this chapter has considered new models of information production emerging from the internet and related technologies. Wikis, blogs, search engines and social networking sites have become part of our everyday lives because the internet has provided an accessible platform for them. In the case of search engines and social networks we have seen valuable new datasets being created as by-products of the primary activity of those services. This final section will explore the challenges by organizations of all sorts as they struggle to make sense of the ever-increasing volumes of data they are generating through their everyday activities. Any organization, particularly those in the private sector, will be amassing data from its external interactions with suppliers, customers, competitors and regulators as well as internally from its employees and business processes. Although companies have kept records of these transactions for centuries, what is new in the 21st century is the quantity and level of detail of this data and the ability to manipulate it for competitive advantage. According to senior IBM executive Ambuj Goyal: 'In the past two or three years we have started to look at information as a strategic capital asset for the organization. This will generate 20, 30 or 40 per cent improvements in the way we run businesses as opposed to the 3 or 5 per cent improvements we achieved before' (Cane, 2009).

IBM has a vested interest in encouraging companies to spend more time and money on information management and analysis as it has spent billions of dollars building analytics centres and employing thousands of staff for this very purpose. However, the fact that organizations have never generated so much data is not in doubt and neither is the growing recognition that developing an understanding of what it all means is increasingly important. It has been estimated that some of the experiments at the Large Hadron Collider at CERN near Geneva generate over 40 terabytes of data a second, far more than can currently be analysed. On a smaller but still significant scale, a typical large supermarket chain sells tens of billions of items a year to millions of customers across hundreds of stores. For example, UK supermarket chain Tesco has over 15 million users of its Clubcard loyalty scheme, which processes approximately 6 million transactions a day. According to Davey (2009) each of these transactions produces 45 different data points requiring Tesco to process over 270 million variables every day as it attempts to make sense of the data its stores are generating. As information technology became embedded in organizations, the volume of data being generated by companies is estimated to be doubling every 12 to 18 months. Davenport, Harris and Morison (2010) argue that this data has real value not only to the organization collecting it but also to third parties that can make use of it. Davenport cites the case of a US supermarket chain that made more money selling its internally generated data to a retail data syndication firm than it did selling meat. The company then went on to admit it made little use of the data beyond putting it on tape, storing it in a mountain, and making sure it was safe from nuclear attack (Davenport, Harris and Morison, 2010, 89).

The growth of these massive, internally generated data sets presents a number of challenges to information professionals, particularly those working in the corporate sector. Traditionally their work has been to manage information that originated from outside their organization, produced by third party publishers. However, the skills needed to classify, organize and disseminate external information do not often translate well to managing data sets of the sort described above. Expertise in computer programming and statistical analysis are often more useful and it is an area that library and information courses might consider incorporating into their curricula. Bentley (2011) believes that organizations are struggling to find the information they need within their own data sets and that information professionals are often those put under pressure to solve this problem. While some new technical capabilities may be needed to address this challenge, many library and information professionals already possess the core skills, according to Hyams (2011a). An understanding of the principles of classification is key to being able to grasp what the issues for the organization are. Quoting Vanda Broughton, an expert in classification and indexing, Hyams makes the case for traditional library and information courses, 'Suddenly, there's an overwhelming amount of information. You might not be able to put structure into it, but having a structured approach, understanding what the problems might be, are really important. It's important to teach [classification] in some depth, because it's only by doing it in some depth that you see why it really matters' (Hyams, 2011a, 23).

Data types

The types of data which organizations are collecting to create these new datasets can be divided into two broad types: structured and unstructured. Structured data typically emerges from transactions that an organization takes part in, such as the purchase and sale of goods. Most products a retailer sells have a unique identifier in the form of a barcode and number. This is used to track the products from their delivery to a central warehouse, then to a specific store, and finally through the checkout when a customer buys it. At the point of sale in many stores the sale of the product is linked to a customer's loyalty card, which allows the retailer to better understand the purchasing habits of its shoppers. In the case of large retailers such as Tesco in the UK and Walmart in the USA, the data is collected in near real time with billions of rows of information added to their datasets every day, according to Babcock (2006). Being able to visualize this much data is difficult and so comparison with a tangible information artefact is useful. It is estimated that Walmart manages approximately 3 petabytes of data which, according to Lyman and Varian (2003), would be equivalent to the contents of 22 US Libraries of Congress or 374 million books.

Bearing in mind that this data is changing hourly, making sense of it and using it to make strategic business decisions presents a challenge. There are companies specializing in data analysis that can do this, drawing on the power of supercomputers to do so. At a relatively mundane level these analyses might help the retailer think about where to position products in a store, based on previous sales and configurations. At a more strategic level they might provide insights into where new stores should be established and help with international expansion. As organizations of all sizes and across many sectors continue to create these new forms of information as by-products of their operations, companies providing the software and hardware to process it are also expanding to the extent that industry analyst IDC estimates that by 2017 the big data sector will be worth US$32.4 billion globally by 2017 (IDC, 2013). It claims that this represents a compound annual growth rate from 2013 to 2017 of 27%, six times the growth rate of the overall information and communication technologies sector.

The above examples relate to the generation of fairly structured sets of data, which scale apart can be processed relatively easily by computers and the software running on them; products and consumers can be given unique identifiers allowing the tracking of purchases and sales. A more recent type of information that organizations are having to understand is less structured and comes in the form of e-mails, recorded phone calls into and out of the organization, and the chatter about their products and services that takes place across the internet on websites and social media. This latter type of information presents some of the greatest challenges, as what people say about you or your company is often beyond your control. Web-based services such as DataSift and Salesforce.com allow subscribers to monitor mentions of specific companies, products and brands across a range of social media in much the same way that press clippings agencies have done through the scanning of newspapers. The main difference between these new services and the press clippings agency is the response times. While press clippings may have been delivered monthly, weekly or even daily, social media monitoring services operate in almost real time and companies with reputations to forge and protect often respond as quickly. Stories that catch the public imagination can spread virally via social media in hours as many companies have found out to their cost. How a company chooses to respond requires careful consideration but not responding is often not a sensible option. Sometimes the problem is of the company's own making, such as when the upmarket UK supermarket Waitrose decided in 2012 to use Twitter to ask customers why they shop at Waitrose. Expecting their happy customers to post positive tweets about the quality of their food the company was shocked when posts such as, 'I shop at Waitrose because their swan burgers are good enough for the Queen' and 'I shop at Waitrose because it makes me feel important and I absolutely detest being surrounded by poor people'. In the end, Waitrose acknowledged the comments were humorous but its marketing team probably wished they had never started the campaign.

Using social media monitoring tools such as those mentioned above, many companies now try to keep track of what current and potential customers are saying about them, and where they can try to add their voice to the conversations. As corporate and brand images become harder to manage and the traditional marketing model of central control is weakened by the decentralized nature of the internet, organizations will have to devote more time to engaging online with their customers.

When everything is connected

While large corporations are finding ways to deal with the new forms of information being produced as by-products of their operations and the 'wild west' that is social media, an even larger contributor to the world of big data is on the horizon, the 'internet of things'. Most of the hardware which we use and which both produces and consumes data over the internet consists of personal computers and other computing devices such as smart phones and tablets. However, as the chips needed to connect devices to the internet become smaller, cheaper and less power-hungry we are starting to see a range of household and industrial devices such as thermostats, smoke alarms, fridges and cars throwing out data. Dormehl (2014) claims that by 2020 there could be 50 billion such devices connected to the internet.

While the practical benefits of some of these connected devices such as fridges and toothbrushes (yes, there is an electric toothbrush which transmits data about how often and the way we brush our teeth) may not be obvious, there are some examples where enormous social and economic advantages may come to pass. One of the world's largest manufacturers of industrial equipment including jet and train engines, GE, is embedding sensors that can transmit information in real time in many of its products. These allow safety-critical data to be analysed as the engines are in use and can alert the company to potential problems before they occur. According to Gertner (2014) a single GE locomotive comprises 200,000 parts, contains 6.7 miles of wiring and contains 250 sensors which transmit 9 million data points every hour. Bearing in mind that over 24,000 locomotives are in use every day in the USA, pulling 365,000 freight cars over 140,000 miles of track, the potential for monitoring this activity via internet-connected sensors becomes apparent. GE claims that wiring up this network and analysing the information which flows from it would allow massive efficiency improvements. Gertner (2014) shows that even a 1% improvement could result in annual savings to the transport companies of US$2.8 billion.

Socially, the potential healthcare benefits are perhaps more exciting than the economic ones described above. Turgeman, Alm and Ratti (2014) believe that by adding sensors to our sewers and toilets we will be able to track the spread of dangerous viruses before they spread to large parts of the population. At a more micro-level, we are already seeing the rapid adoption of personal, wearable devices such as Fitbits and smart watches, as well as health apps on our smart phones, which are measuring users' blood pressure, heart rate and other indicators. Google's purchase of Nest Labs, a maker of smart thermostats and fire alarms, in 2014 for over US$3 billion has brought the notion of the smart house a little closer even if it has raised concerns over the internet giant knowing even more about us. Privacy issues aside, this information if collected and analysed on a mass scale would provide medical researchers with unprecedented insights into the relationship between our health, lifestyle and the effectiveness of different treatments.

Data as the new currency

As industries face the challenge of adapting to the digital world, some more successfully than others, so too are governments. The main challenge for many industries has been adapting their business models to ones which allow them to continue making profits when information, which used to be a scarce resource, is freely available and replicable at near zero cost. This has also made it more difficult for authoritarian regimes to control information flows and threatened their monopolies on national communication systems. Other governments have seen the digital revolution as an opportunity to provide more efficient services by allowing interactions between citizens and the state to take place online, removing some of the friction that exists in the realm of paper and physical spaces.

Perhaps a new form of information promises, or threatens, far greater social and economic changes than we have seen so far. Digital currencies such as Bitcoin have the potential to render many of the traditional functions of the state such as managing the money supply through national currencies obsolete. Bitcoin is the leader of this vanguard of new currencies and is based on open source software. It is a virtual currency in that there is no physical equivalent such as US dollar bills or UK pound coins and exists only in the realm of the so-called 'public ledger' that exists on multiple computers and tracks the creation and exchange of Bitcoins as they are used in transactions. The currency is controversial because of its use in illegal financial transactions for drugs, weapons and other suspect activities; nonetheless, a growing number of legitimate businesses will accept Bitcoins in exchange for their products and services. These include hotels, restaurants and high-profile companies such as the Chicago Sun-Times, OKCupid and Dell. How many transactions these companies actually make using Bitcoins is unclear and for some companies accepting Bitcoins is a marketing stunt to show they are at the leading edge of new technologies. However, as the currency becomes more acceptable and offers benefits such as lower transaction fees and relative anonymity, it is possible it may become a serious challenger to national currencies. Since 2010 the value of a Bitcoin has been volatile, growing from nothing to almost US$1000 in late 2013 and at the time of writing in August 2014 sits at just under US$600.

Whether Bitcoin succeeds or is eclipsed by another virtual currency is largely irrelevant. An industry has sprung up alongside the currency allowing anyone to buy and sell it as well as software to manage the digital wallets users need to manage their Bitcoins. As a proof of concept it is apparent that a new global currency can be created which bypasses national banks, treasuries and international banking agreements, which regulate and track the flows of financial transactions. Some states, notably the USA and China, have tried to crack down on Bitcoin exchanges and the online markets such as Silk Road, which relied on the currency to provide anonymity for the many illegal sales of drugs and weapons that took place there, but it could be argued that the genie is out of the bottle. In a world where most information has been digitized it is only natural that currencies, which are usually not based on anything more than a trust in the authority of the nation state, should follow. Perhaps, as some commentators have suggested, Bitcoin is not something to be overly concerned about and we should think of it as a natural evolution of the internet, as the TCP/IP (Transmission Control Protocol and the Internet Protocol) of money.

Concluding comments

This chapter has considered how new technologies, in particular mass computing and the internet, are leading to new models by which information is produced. These are presenting new opportunities for innovation, business creation and social advancement. As the technologies that are leading these changes become cheaper and more widespread, their effects will be magnified. The next chapter will explore the next stage in the information value chain and look at the new ways we are storing information and some of the challenges they present to information professionals, traditionally the guardians of such assets.

3
New models of information storage

Introduction

Societies that had no way of codifying information relied on the human memory and storytelling as the only way to share information and to pass it down to future generations. A number of myths and legends that are now part of our literature and culture are likely to have originated from what is called the oral tradition. By the nature of such memorized story-telling it is often impossible to ascertain where stories originate but it is likely that the legend of Beowulf and the poems of Homer started life in this way. The development of the cuneiform writing system over 5000 years ago and subsequent alphabets that we would now recognize enabled information to be transcribed for the first time and provided one of the cornerstones for the emergence of what we would call civilization. Financial imperatives drove much of the innovation in writing methods as traders needed to document their purchases and sales and public officials took note of taxes which were due or had been paid. That we know anything about these early alphabets is because many of them were written into clay tablets, which have lasted through the millennia. Apart from the development of new media such as parchment and paper for storing texts, the evolution of writing tools such as pencils and pens and then the invention of the printing press to make the reproduction of documents more efficient, little else has changed since the first clay tablets of 3000 BC.

The inventions mentioned above were undoubtedly significant, particularly the printing press, but the final output was always the same: a physical, analogue representation of the information. While typewriters and printing presses allowed books, newspapers and other documents to be created at ever lower costs and in larger numbers, what came out of the machine was still something with weight and volume that degraded over time and required physical space to be stored. Much of the work of librarians over the last several hundred years has been the management of these physical resources, which has required shelving, storage repositories and the replacement and rotation of stock as it wears out or becomes outdated. Digital information is not subject to many of these limitations as it has no significant physical footprint and does not wear out in the traditional sense. However many times a digital document is read, copied and shared the integrity of its content is not impaired.

Apart from printed formats, information has been stored in other analogue formats such as phonograph cylinders, gramophone records and audio and video tapes. Like books these storage media took up considerable physical space and, unlike digital formats, were subject to degradation in quality and integrity the more they were copied. With the advent of the first computers in the 1940s, one of the primary aims of computer scientists was to develop new ways of storing the data that the computers required for processing as well as their outputs. Punch cards similar to those previously used by player pianos and weaving looms of the 19th century were the primary storage medium for computers until replaced by magnetic tape and then the disc drives we are familiar with today. The early computers of the 1950s weighed hundreds of kilograms, cost millions of pounds in today's money and could store less than a five-thousandth of the data held in a standard smart phone of 2015. Apart from increases in the capacity of modern computer storage, the fall in price is equally dramatic: a megabyte of storage in the mid-1950s cost approximately £125,000 in today's money while a megabyte in 2015 costs less than 0.003 pence. As Levie (2011) points out, by 2020 businesses will have to deal with 50 times the amount of data they did in 2011: 'Our software, infrastructure, and organizations are ill-prepared to manage this scale of data creation, let alone generate anything meaningful or useful with this amount of content being created and shared.' This chapter will explore the implications of these changes for the way we manage information in the 21st century and what it means for the organizations and individuals that produce and consume the ever-increasing streams of digital bits.

Preserving the internet

Over 2000 years ago the Great Library of Alexandria held the greatest collection of manuscripts ever gathered from around the world. It was a bold attempt to capture the knowledge of the ancient world through recognition of the power of codified information. Phillips (2010) points to the aggressive acquisition strategy of the library's keepers that eventually led to a collection of between 400,000 and 700,000 items. As significant as the unprecedented size of the library itself are the tales of its destruction. How the Great Library and its many scrolls and books eventually met their end is a matter of debate but the fact of their disappearance is not. Either through fire, vandalism or theft, this priceless collection was lost to the world, never to be reassembled again. Parallels have been drawn with the internet and the, often transient, information that is dispersed across web servers around the world.

In many countries, publishers are legally obliged to deposit at least one copy of every book and magazine they produce with public repositories, often the national library. Until very recently this has resulted in comprehensive archives of mainstream printed materials and given us a series of modern-day equivalents of the Great Library of Alexandria. However, the rise of digital forms of information has presented challenges to these endeavours. The web as a publishing platform makes the creation of a single repository for publications almost impossible. Web pages are particularly transient and often have a very limited life-span. Dellavalle et al. (2003) point out the dangers of relying on the permanence of web links when referencing materials. Their research in the USA showed that almost 20% of the URLs used in a high school science curriculum became inactive between August 2002 and March 2003. More recently, Prithviraj and Kumar (2014) have shown that just over half of the URLs in the papers for a large collection of conference proceedings published between 2001 and 2010 were dead by 2013.

Much of the value we derive from the web is based on the free linking between information resources but this is also a fundamental weakness as websites can be taken down as easily as they were created in the first place. As new web formats emerge such as blogs, wikis and other content management publishing systems, keeping track of who is publishing what and preserving their outputs is increasingly difficult. In the 1990s when the web was still in its infancy, Yahoo!'s directory of websites based around subject areas was the starting point for many researchers seeking information. This subject-based approach to organizing the web may seem rather quaint now but it was a useful resource when websites were counted in the hundreds of thousands and not the hundreds of millions as they are today. In 2010 Yahoo! closed its European directory sites as it became impossible to update and maintain such resource-hungry operations and in 2014 announced it would be closing its US directory by the end of that year (Sullivan, 2014). The DMOZ open directory is now the only, as of late 2014, major web directory. Although, like Yahoo! before it, DMOZ does not host the websites it links to, it does at least provide a snapshot of the web in terms of the breadth of content contained within it. However, as web pages disappear they provide no backup of those resources in the way that a national archive does.

Although books go out of print we are usually able to locate a copy in the British Library, the Library of Congress or whatever institution in our country is charged with maintaining such a resource. Is anyone doing the same for the internet?

Luckily for those concerned about the disappearance of web pages the answer is a qualified yes. Since 1996 the Internet Archive in the USA has been archiving websites and making them available to internet users through its Wayback Machine, a freely accessible resource that allows anyone to look at previous versions of websites. The Internet Archive is a non-profit organization and has no legal rights to oblige owners of web pages to lodge copies of their materials with it, but with the support of grants and donations from individuals and charities it has amassed the world's largest repository of web pages. According to its website, in May 2014 it had collected almost 10 petabytes (approximately 400 billion web pages) of information spread across four data centres and this was growing at a rate of 100,000 gigabytes of information a month. The driving force behind the Internet Archive is Brewster Kahle who, although not a librarian by profession, embodies some of the key characteristics of any successful library and information professional. He was even described in a 2009 article in *The Economist* as 'the internet's librarian' (Economist, 2009). Kahle himself draws parallels between the objectives of his archive and those of the Great Library of Alexandria, with the Internet Archive making the following claim on its 'About' page: 'Libraries exist to preserve society's cultural artefacts and to provide access to them. If libraries are to continue to foster education and scholarship in this era of digital technology, it's essential for them to extend those functions into the digital world' (Internet Archive, 2014).

Despite its best endeavours, the Internet Archive can only ever offer snapshots in time of the state of the web, with many pages never being indexed because they were changed before the archive visited them, were never found in the first place or lay behind password-protected firewalls. It is inevitable that much of what is published on the web will never be preserved and will disappear into digital darkness. While it could be argued that much of this lost information was of such a trivial nature that its demise will be no loss to humanity, it could equally be said that what seems trivial and unimportant now may have a significance to future generations that we cannot yet comprehend. It is often the diaries of everyday folk or informal personal photographs that tell us more about our past than official records. Although the Internet Archive is an attempt to capture web resources on a global scale it should be noted that a number of smaller, more local initiatives are under way to build digital archives, and some of these are considered later in this chapter.

The Internet Archive is a public-spirited attempt to store digital information for the benefit of current and future generations and maintains a significant technical infrastructure to hold this information securely. In the for-profit sector there are far larger investments being made to capture and store the data that drives the web. As the world's most popular search engine, Google is at the forefront of these attempts to index the web. Google is reticent about releasing data on its operations, but in 2012 the company revealed that it had indexed more than 30 trillion unique URLs, 30,000 times larger than the index of 1 billion pages it created in 2000 (Sullivan, 2012b). The underlying infrastructure of the big internet companies is usually kept secret for commercial reasons, but in 2011 it was revealed that approximately 900,000 servers were powering Google's operations, consuming an estimated 0.01% of the world's electricity (Miller, 2011). Finding low-cost and reliable sources of energy to power and cool its data centres is an ongoing challenge for Google, which is investing hundreds of millions of dollars in solar and wind farms, and building centres next to the sea and in the Arctic Circle where cooling can be done naturally. Although Google manages the most web servers, other internet companies are not too far behind in their requirements for computer storage. Facebook's more than 1.3 billion users had by late 2013 uploaded more than 250 billion photos to the site and were adding more at a rate of almost 350 million per day (Wagner, 2013). The data storage requirements for these companies are unprecedented in the history of computing.

How organizations store information

The previous section examined how, for different reasons, the Internet Archive and Google are attempting to store web pages and associated data on a global scale. This section moves down to the organizational level and considers how our public and private bodies are managing their digital data. As most of the information that we deal with in our daily work lives is becoming digital it is a growing challenge for organizations to manage it in a way that is secure, compliant with legal requirements and readily accessible to employees, regulators and other stakeholders as and when they need it. Information has moved out of filing cabinets and bookshelves and onto personal computers, file servers, memory sticks, smart phones and content management systems.

Academia

Universities and colleges of higher education have long been one of the primary producers of original research materials that have been the basis for many world-changing innovations. The founders of Google, Larry Page and Sergey Brin, were students at Stanford University in the USA when their research project involved the creation of a web crawler that formed the foundation of the Google search engine. The key channels for disseminating academic research findings are the peer-reviewed journals that cover academic disciplines from archaeology to zoology with titles such as *Celestial Mechanics and Dynamical Astronomy* and *Journal of Phenomenological Psychology*. While these journals are still the primary method for academics to present their research there is a trend for academic institutions to host their research outputs in their own online institutional repositories that are accessible via the internet.

In a world where anyone with an internet connection can distribute their own digital content without the need for editorial control and the permission of an established publisher, it seems logical that universities should also be able to join in. Peer-reviewed journals and conference proceedings are often expensive for users to access and prevent potentially useful information gaining a wider distribution. This has encouraged the deployment of institutional digital repositories by many universities (see case study below), which are making research findings accessible over the public web. Lynch (2003, 2) offers a broad but useful definition of what he sees as the key characteristics of an institutional repository: 'a university-based institutional repository is a set of services that a university offers to the members of its community for the management and dissemination of digital materials created by the institution and its community members. . . . An institutional repository is not simply a fixed set of software and hardware'. For academic librarians, the development of institutional repositories presents both challenges and opportunities. Some of these challenges centre on the acquisition and maintenance of new technical skills required to help specify, design and implement these new systems. Because of the nature of their core skills in managing information, librarians are well placed to play an active role in these tasks. However, as with the deployment of other technical innovations in organizations, there is the potential for tension between library and information professionals and IT staff over who is responsible for making key decisions. Newton, Miller and Stowell Bracke describe the skills required by academic librarians to lead the deployment of institutional repositories and argue that such information professionals may indeed 'find themselves building or strengthening relationships with disciplinary faculty and research centres on campus while extending the boundaries of library service' (Newton, Miller and Stowell Bracke, 2011, 54).

Once the institutional repository is up and running the next task is to keep it populated with the latest research outputs from academic researchers in the institution. As with many content management systems in all types of organizations, this is an ongoing challenge. Assuming that because a system has been set up to hold research materials it will automatically be used in that way is a mistake.

Without the right incentives most people will not be inclined, for reasons of time or plain laziness, to upload materials. Carrot and stick approaches can be used to encourage positive behaviours. Carrot approaches might be to demonstrate to users the benefits of having their outputs exposed to a wider audience or offering rewards for regular uploaders. A more stringent stick might be applied in the form of contractual obligations to place materials on the institutional repository or the withholding of research funding for non-compliance.

It is worth noting that one of the advantages an institutional repository offers over the traditional academic publishing model is the variety of file types and formats it can hold. The peer-reviewed journal paper is still the gold standard for evaluating the work of an academic, but institutional repositories allow other types of outputs to be stored and distributed to a wide audience. These may include working papers, presentations, videos and original data sets. There is a danger of the institutional repository containing too much trivial information and this is where the skills of the information professional may be needed to sift through the noise of digital artefacts and find the nuggets of valuable information. Just as Google has helped internet users find the information they need from hundreds of millions of websites through its PageRank algorithm, so new tools such as OAIster and Google Scholar are being developed to index and help people find the academic outputs they require from institutional repositories (Stevenson and Hodges, 2008). It will be increasingly important for institutional repositories to be found and indexed by such services if they are to remain visible and relevant to the research community. The use of common file formats and readable metadata play an important role in this respect as does the co-operation between academic institutions, research funding bodies, search companies and publishers. Woodward and Estelle (2010) point out that as long as the institutional repository complies with the Open Archives Initiative Protocol for Metadata Harvesting, any item should be discoverable by commonly used web search engines.

CASE STUDY DSPACE INSTITUTIONAL REPOSITORY SOFTWARE

DSpace emerged in 2002 from a partnership between the Massachusetts Institute of Technology (MIT) and Hewlett-Packard and is now the most widely used open source software of this type globally. As the software began to be adopted by research institutions around the world, it was felt a more formal arrangement was needed to guide future development resulting in the creation of the DSpace Foundation in 2007. In 2009 a merger with the Fedora Commons initiative led to the forming of not-for-profit Duraspace, which with its community members coordinates the evolution of the DSpace software. Institutions using DSpace include Harvard University and Yale University in the USA, Imperial College and the London School of Economics in the UK, and the University of Adelaide and University of Sydney in Australia, and more than 1500 other research institutions around the world. Because DSpace is open source and has attracted a large community of developers, it is highly adaptable and allows users to customize installations to suit the needs of their organizations. The software can store multimedia contents such as audio and video files, as well as traditional text-based documents. Recently DSpace and other institutional repository software providers and developers have improved the way that search engines can index their contents to shows up in search results. This presents a potentially interesting evolution in the design and deployment of academic repositories as they seek to gain the attention of internet searchers by appearing more highly in their search results.

Just as academic institutions are exploiting cheap data storage and an open web to share the outputs of their research to a wider audience, so too are private enterprises building large-scale data centres to house a wide range of digital information. These data centres may be used for reasons of competitive advantage and/or for legal requirements where data retention is important to comply with financial legislation. The scale of some of these initiatives is forcing innovations in data security, storage capacity and energy use.

Legal requirements

Until recently public bodies were generally legally required to maintain records for fixed periods of time. This information was typically the output of administrative bodies as they carried out the work of the executive and legislative parts of government. In the UK the Public Record Office Act of 1838 was passed to 'keep safely the public records' and has been amended over the years, most recently in 2010 with the Constitutional Reform and Governance Act. Similar legislation exists at state and national levels in most developed economies where obligations are placed on public bodies over how long data must be retained, and the access rights to those documents by the general public. Over the last several decades legislation on document retention has also extended to private companies, a trend that has accelerated since 2000 following financial scandals and fears over terrorist activities.

In the USA the collapse of Enron and WorldCom, and other corporate failures due to financial malpractice in the late 1990s and early 2000s, led the US Congress to pass the Sarbanes-Oxley Act, which placed more stringent financial accounting obligations on publicly quoted companies. As well as applying to US corporations it also extends to foreign owned companies that have listings on the US stock market. The Act has been criticized by many companies because of the increased costs it imposes on them through compliance with the new accounting rules and the obligation for public companies to store internally generated information for periods of up to seven years. According to Kidd (2003), over 10,000 separate laws in the USA deal with document and data retention but the Sarbanes-Oxley Act places the most onerous obligations on companies. In the UK, the data consulting firm Watson Hall (2014) lists 38 different types of data that organizations, public and private, are required to retain for periods of between four days and 50 years, and in some cases indefinitely. The types of data described by Watson Hall include e-mails, personnel records, web activity and telephone records. Some of this information is in paper format and stored in the traditional sense but increasingly it is digital, requiring new skills and procedures on the part of those responsible for its maintenance.

Where information is paper-based there are physical objects that cannot be ignored and in some respects their retention is easier than less tangible digital data. Accidentally wiping a hard disc drive is easily done so procedures need to be in place to maintain audits of electronic information along with instructions for backing it up to secure locations. The fragility of digital data was highlighted in 2007 when a computer technician from the Alaskan tax office accidentally erased a disc drive containing an account worth US$38 billion while carrying out routine maintenance work (Maxcer, 2007). When the tape backups of the data were found to be unreadable, staff in the department had to rescan and enter data stored in over 300 cardboard boxes, which cost US$200,000 in overtime payments. Although this example may be at the extreme end of data storage problems, it illustrates both the temporal nature of digital data and the value of paper backups. However, it is not practical for most organizations to maintain both forms.

Although the Sarbanes-Oxley Act in the USA and other similar legislation around the world are aimed at preventing illegal accounting practices in corporations, other legislation has been enacted in the wake of terrorist activities in the USA and Europe. This is having implications for telephone and internet companies and forcing them to store ever-increasing amounts of information about their customers for longer periods of time. After the 2001 attacks on New York City and Washington DC and the 2005 bombings in London there was a concern that telephone and e-mail communications between the attackers were not being stored by internet and telecommunications providers to allow investigations by the security services. In Europe this was driven by the European Union Data Retention Directive of 2006 and in the USA by the Patriot Act of 2001. Both these pieces of legislation place responsibilities on telecommunication and internet service providers (ISPs) for keeping customer records and providing access when required to official bodies. However, a strong signal was sent in early 2014 that legislators, in Europe at least, might be pushing back against what many see as draconian surveillance legislation. In April 2014, the European Court of Justice ruled that the European Union Data Retention Directive was invalid on the basis that it interfered with the fundamental rights to respect for private life and to the protection of personal data. In their ruling the judges stated, 'The fact that data are retained and subsequently used without the subscriber or registered user being informed is likely to generate in the minds of the person concerned the feeling that their private lives are the subject of constant surveillance' (Vierstraete, 2014).

The concerns of the European Court of Justice echo the notions of surveillance and control developed by the French philosopher Michel Foucault in the 1970s and 1980s. Foucault (1977) studied the development of prisons and other public institutions such as schools and hospitals and the way they were designed to create 'docile bodies'; citizens who would perform appropriately in the emerging industrial societies of the 18th and 19th centuries. Foucault discussed the work of the utilitarian, early 19th century philosopher Jeremy Bentham and his designs for a modern prison. Bentham's design for a 'reforming' prison he called the Panopticon relied on a central tower from which guards could see into each prison cell but could not themselves be observed. He believed this would have the effect of placing uncertainty in the minds of prisoners as to when they were being watched and lead to a self-regulating form of behaviour, which over time would reform the character of the inmates. It is interesting that the European Court of Justice saw the European Union Data Retention Directive in a similar light whereby internet and telecommunication users would never be sure who might be looking at their online activities.

According to Vierstraete (2014) the EU's ruling means that the directive is now invalid, which will have implications for those EU member states that had implemented it within their own national legal systems, the UK being one of them. As a response to this, in July 2014 the UK government rushed a piece of legislation through Parliament known as the Data Retention and Investigatory Powers Act (DRIP). This was controversial not just for the speed with which it was enacted and the lack of public debate but also because it is seen by many as extending the power of the state to force internet and telecommunication companies to store personal data on their users. One of the responses to the legislation was an open letter to the House of Commons by 15 academic technology law experts. In the letter they state,

> The legislation goes far beyond simply authorising data retention in the UK. In fact, Drip attempts to extend the territorial reach of the British interception powers, expanding the UK's ability to mandate the interception of communications content across the globe. It introduces powers that are not only completely novel in the United Kingdom, they are some of the first of their kind globally.   (Kiss, 2014)

There are strong arguments on both sides of this debate where the need for national security has to be weighed against personal rights to privacy, and the implications for the companies which manage our internet connectivity are significant. Until recently their main interest in storing details of our online activities has been for billing and marketing purposes. As we spend increasing amounts of our lives online the data generated has increased enormously so ISPs have only tended to store as little data as was needed to deliver the services their customers had paid for. Having to keep all data relating to customer activity for up to several years is a significant undertaking. The media regulator Ofcom estimates that in 2013 in the UK over 225 billion minutes of voice conversations were carried across the networks, 130 billion texts were sent and over 1 trillion e-mails exchanged on top of over 800 million gigabytes of web traffic (Ofcom, 2014). The logistics for the carriers of having to store details of those communications, including every website that a customer visits, for up to two years, is considerable. In Austria it was calculated that the cost to ISPs of compliance with the European Union Data Retention Directive could be up to €20 million a year, a considerable sum for companies operating in a highly competitive market (Libbenga, 2011).

   Apart from the issues surrounding personal privacy of such granular data being stored and the costs mentioned above, the logistics of storing such massive volumes of data in a format that allows it to be searched and possibly retrieved on demand is presenting substantial technical challenges. While storing such information is seen by many organizations as a burden that reduces profits, a large number of businesses are investing large sums to build databases for purely commercial reasons. The following section considers the growth in data mining that is driving attempts to better understand customer behaviour and many of the other variables that affect business performance.

Data mining

In Chapter 2 we saw that as companies generate ever-increasing amounts of data from their operations they increasingly see these new information streams as sources of competitive advantage. Retailers are a good example of this trend where large supermarkets such as Tesco in the UK (see case study below) and Walmart in the USA typically sell thousands of product lines to millions of customers every day. Keeping track of these transactions is essential to make sure that products are replaced on the shelves in a timely manner but the data generated also provides some valuable insights into customer behaviour, which can help increase sales and profits. The value of this data was highlighted by the US retailer Sears in 2013, when it revealed it was converting some of its retail stores into data centres to store the information assets it was producing (Ryan, 2013).

CASE STUDY The Tesco Clubcard

The Tesco Clubcard was introduced by UK supermarket chain Tesco in 1995 and currently has over 15 million members. The Clubcard offers an incentive for shoppers to shop at Tesco as points are accumulated based on how much is spent and these are then translated into discount vouchers for future shopping visits, but the real value of the Clubcard lies in the data it generates for Tesco. Each time the card is scanned at the checkout it tells the company which products were bought and matches that to the card owner. Before the Clubcard, Tesco knew which products were being sold but did not know who was buying them. When shoppers apply for the loyalty card they are asked to give details about who else lives in their household, and their age, gender and so on. This data combined with their home address and the products they buy allows Tesco to build up a very rich picture of its shoppers. Other retailers offer similar schemes such as the Nectar card scheme in the UK, which is used by a number of different companies, and the My Best Buy program in the USA. These schemes generate huge amounts of data about shoppers' buying habits and allow retailers to better understand their customers by looking for patterns in purchase behaviour. In a sign that Tesco wants to expand its loyalty program it is now tailoring the advertisements which customers see when watching Clubcard TV, an internet television channel run by Tesco, based on the products they purchase in store.

Large data centres are generally the preserve of global internet companies such as Google and Amazon and other large corporations, but it is important to note that companies of all sizes are placing greater emphasis on the value of their data assets. Large retailers such as Walmart and Tesco provide obvious examples of this trend but it also applies to smaller companies that can leverage their data to compete more effectively. One of the constraints facing small and medium-sized enterprises (SMEs) has been the cost of managing data centres and the lack of knowledge of what to do with the data once it is captured. Just as the internet has made it easier for new entrants to the retail sector to compete with established players through e-commerce, so too is the same technology providing new sources of data to evaluate and low-cost tools to perform the analysis. Budnarowska and Marciniak (2009) show how a free tool such as Google Analytics can help small online retailers better understand how visitors to their websites behave and the factors that lead to actual sales. Other low-cost online tools such as Salesforce.com and Insightly also offer powerful applications for customer relationship management that have previously been the domain of large companies. One of the key differences apart from the price is that the data is not stored by the companies themselves but is accessed via the internet and managed by the service providers. This cloud-based approach to application and data access is allowing SMEs to use data management services that were previously unaffordable.

Figure 3.1 is a simplified version of the key stages involved in data mining and can be applied across a range of organizational types. Although the focus of data mining activities has traditionally been in the commercial sector and security services, it also has relevance to many public organizations including libraries of all types. Just as a retailer is concerned with maximizing efficiencies in the way it purchases, displays and sells stock, so too libraries need to ensure they hold the titles their patrons want, in sufficient quantities and in the right locations. Local library services do not have the same budget for these activities as Walmart or Tesco, but there are ways they can engage in understanding customer data that do not cost the earth. Broady-Preston and Felice (2006) describe some tentative steps taken by the University of

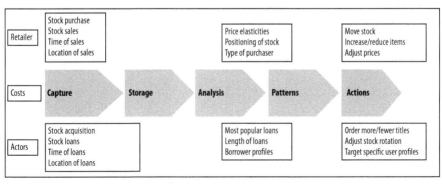

Figure 3.1 Data mining activities for retailers and libraries

Malta library service to develop better relationships with the users through a customer relationship management system, with mixed results. Wang (2007) points to resistance on the part of staff in implementing a customer relationship management system in an academic library but describes the benefits that can accrue if the system is carefully thought through. Libraries are certainly able to generate enough data on their operations and customers to populate a customer relationship management system including data on stock held, items loaned, activity of users, loan lengths and activity on their websites. With financial pressures on library staff, public and academic, likely to increase over the coming years, developing a better understanding of users, their habits and requirements will become a more important task. Maintaining and analysing records of these activities and preferences will play an important part in this.

Collection digitization

The customer relationship management activities described above will play an increasing role in the jobs of many library staff and put pressures on the data they are required to store but the collections they manage and provide access to will always be at the core of their responsibilities. Woodward and Estelle (2010) point out that although Google is probably the single largest creator of digital assets through its Google Books project and other initiatives, individual libraries are also actively engaged in digitizing their collections. They describe the US Library of Congress's US$2 million project to digitize old, brittle books and the £22 million digitization programme funded by the Joint Information Systems Committee (JISC) in the UK, which encompasses old sound recordings, newspapers and cartoons.

In the UK the British Library has been active in creating and offering access to digital versions of its printed collections. By late 2011, the Library was offering access via its website to over 4 million digital items and 40 million pages (British Library, 2011). In a sign of the inevitable move to digital content creation and curation, the chief executive of the British Library, Dame Lynne Brindley, said in 2010:

> By the year 2020 we estimate that only 25% of all titles worldwide will be published in print form alone. 75% will only be published digitally, or in both digital and print form. Our research suggests that as use of mobile devices become ubiquitous, users will expect seamless access to information and services, and will assume that everything is available on the web.
>
> (Rossini, 2010)

As well as preparing for the storage of future digital content, the British Library is also creating digital versions of much of its analogue archive of books, newspapers, magazines and other collections. In 2011 it announced a joint project with Google to digitize 250,000 out-of-copyright books, pamphlets and periodicals from the period 1700 to 1870. This and other digitization projects by the British Library are presenting significant challenges to its technical infrastructure as it needs to store and then provide access to the archive content. In order to maintain the security of the archives all content is mirrored across two sites so that if one site was to suffer a disaster the other would hold a copy of the many hundreds of terabytes of data so far collected. The British Library continues to be at the forefront of innovations in the digitization of collections with the aim of making them more accessible to researchers. In 2014 a joint venture between the British Library, the Department of Computer Science at University College London (UCL) and the UCL Centre for Digital Humanities was set up to open up digital artefacts in the arts and humanities collection (Baker, 2014). The British Library Big Data Experiment project is one of a number of initiatives by the British Library which promise to combine computer science applications of big data analysis with user-friendly front-ends, which will extend the reach of the organization from its main building in central London.

Digitizing collections offers many advantages to the curators and those looking for information across the archives. Space savings and the absences of worries about the effects of time and humidity on paper resources are obvious benefits as is the ease with which digital collections can be indexed and searched. However, while paper and ink are universally accessible and readable forms of information representation that are capable of lasting centuries under the right conditions, digital files may not be so robust. It is understood that digital storage media such as hard drives and optical discs have limited life spans but as long as the data they contain is frequently copied over to fresh media then problems of degradation can be avoided. This is helped by the fact that digital copies are faithful duplicates of the original artefacts, unlike in the analogue world where excessive copying can result in lower quality backups. A photocopy of a photocopy is an example of the weakness in relying on analogue backups. The main issue for digital archive managers is making sure that the formats in which the data is encoded is one which future generations will be able to make sense of. Many of us still have videocassette recorders in our homes but because we moved to the DVD format for video entertainment over the previous decade, it will become increasingly difficult to play our old video cassettes. As video streaming over the internet becomes more popular through services such as Netflix, our DVDs are likely to go the same way as video cassettes. A digital archive will be of little use if nobody in 100 years has the ability to decode and understand the files it contains.

An example of a digital collection much less than 100 years old that faced this issue is the Domesday Project undertaken by the BBC in 1986 to mark the 900th anniversary of William the Conqueror's land survey of England in the 11th century. The project involved the collation of text and video submissions from schools and members of the public onto video discs to present a snapshot of life in Britain in the mid-1980s. However, only 15 years later it had become almost impossible to find the hardware capable of reading the discs as they were in a format that had not been successful. The US space agency NASA has had similar problems with image and video tapes from its space missions in the 1960s and 1970s. Some of the tapes were in formats that required machines to be built from scratch to decode them. Can anyone be confident that the JPG format for pictures, the Audio Video Interleaved (AVI) format for video or the PDF format for documents will be readable by our grandchildren in 2030?

To prevent us falling into a digital dark age so-called techno-archaeologists offer solutions to decode unreadable digital files using rebuilt machines and software emulators which can read dead formats within contemporary systems. A more sustainable solution is to create standards and formats which will be readable for generations to come by using agreed common protocols and frameworks for encoding. A number of organizations and research projects are now addressing this issue. The Born Digital project, funded by the Andrew W. Mellon Foundation and comprising members from the universities of Hull in the UK and Stanford, Yale and Virginia in the USA, is a good example. Running from 2009 to 2011, the project aimed to 'create an inter-institutional framework for stewarding born-digital content' (University of Virginia Library, 2011). In addition to devising systems for helping organizations preserve their digital content in accessible formats, the project members looked at ways to ensure that important metadata is not stripped out when digital items are converted from one format to another. It is important to remember that the visible manifestation of such items is not the only facet required for preservation. For example, the metadata associated with digital images and which is seldom seen by those viewing them often includes the time and date the image was taken, the device that took it and, increasingly, where the image was taken through the use of geo tags. Valuable metadata associated with documents can include date of creation, authors, version number and indexing terms. As digital collections grow this peripheral information will become increasingly important for information professionals who wish to make sense of their archives.

It is not just document and image collections which are now being digitized;

recent developments in 3D scanning are now enabling physical objects to be digitally captured and then made available to view via the internet. The Smithsonian Institution in the USA, which manages 19 museums and nine research centres is at the leading edge of 3D scanning of artefacts and aims to digitize its entire collection in this way. However, the challenge of this undertaking is not insignificant and will require new processes and workflows if it is to be realized. The Director of the Smithsonian Digital Program Office, Gunter Waibel, outlines the work that lies ahead for his team: 'at 137 million objects, artworks and specimens, capturing the entire collection at a rate of 1 item per minute would take over 260 years of 24/7 effort' (Waibel, 2014).

Keeping it all safe

Information professionals responsible for managing their organization's information know the importance of data security whether to protect against attempts by outsiders to hack into systems or to prevent natural disasters from destroying such resources. At a basic level, processes can be put in place to make sure regular backups are made of important data and that these backup copies are spread across a range of locations. However, sometimes this is not perceived to be sufficient, particularly for organizations that rely on their information resources as their prime source of competitive advantage. Technology and pharmaceutical companies, for example, rely on their research to develop new products and drugs and make significant investments to ensure their competitors are not aware of their strategic plans. These companies go to great lengths to lock down sensitive data through restricting internal access and securing it against networked attacks.

A recent trend for companies wishing to provide physical security to their data has been to collocate it in secure underground stores, typically ex-nuclear bunkers and abandoned mines. The US company Iron Mountain offers such facilities with its main secure premises located in 1.7 million square feet under a mountain in Pennsylvania. One of the advantages of the 200-foot-deep mine with its own natural underwater lake is that it remains at a constant temperature of 13°C, which negates the need for expensive cooling systems that above-ground data centres require to prevent the computer servers from over-heating. According to Miller (2013) more than 2700 people work in the Iron Mountain facility, which has its own restaurant, water treatment plant, fire engines and backup power systems. Also in the USA, the Mountain Complex is almost twice the size of Iron Mountain and is built into the side of a mountain, which its owners claim is setting 'the gold standard in secure storage' (Mountain Complex, nd). Whether such sites really offer the security their clients require is debatable as information security breaches are often caused by dishonest or careless employees, but putting a data centre in a mountain certainly gives the impression of security and gives a new meaning to the term 'data mining'.

Storage at the personal level

Until recently the data that we personally managed typically comprised physical items such as photographs, letters, CDs, DVDs, books and possibly some old school reports and diaries. Spread across shelves and some dusty boxes in the attic, they were easy to manage and followed us as we moved house. Our photographs are now dispersed across memory cards, personal computers, mobile phones and social media sites. Personal correspondence may be in multiple accounts and, like photos, may reside on ours and other people's social media pages. There is a similar story for our music and increasingly books, as e-readers such as the Amazon Kindle and tablet computers become platforms for media consumption. Keeping track of all this information is not easy, particularly when devices such as smart phones, computers and MP3 players are replaced at ever-shortening intervals. Love letters, once treasured and kept for years, are now rather more transient in their digital format and may disappear as soon as you upgrade your computer or switch e-mail provider. With the rise of messaging apps such as Snapchat, transient takes on a new meaning as messages are deleted within seconds of the recipient seeing them. Keeping track of all this data and making sure it is backed up and preserved for posterity is forcing many of us to adopt practices that have been the preserve of digital archivists. Some organizations are already anticipating the rise in demand for these services such as the non-profit foundation Chronicle of Life, which promises to look after your digital memories 'forever'. The foundation's charges are significantly higher than more mainstream cloud storage services such as Dropbox; it charges a one-off fee of US$100 for enough storage for 250 photos.

Table 3.1 presents an overview of some of the media devices commonly found in most households, and their characteristics. It summarizes some of the core media devices we use in our daily lives and the formats typically used to create and present the data. It demonstrates the complexity of competing standards, some open and some proprietary, that we have to consider when working out a preservation plan for it all. It is not unreasonable to assume that a typical family with children may have produced several thousand gigabytes of digital data over a ten-year period. Video would probably make up the bulk of this with an hour of video from a modern consumer camcorder requiring approximately 4 gigabytes of storage. Finding the hardware to store our personal digital archives is

Table 3.1 Personal data storage devices			
Media	**Device**	**Capacity**	**Format**
Music	iPod or MP3 player Smart phone CD player	700MB–128GB	MP3 AAC WAV CDA Vorbis WMA
Photographs	Digital camera Smart phone Tablet computer	2–128GB	JPEG TIFF RAW
Video	Video camera Smart phone Web cam	2–128GB	H.264 MPEG 1,2,4 MJPEG WMV
Text	Personal computer E-book reader Tablet computer	2GB–1TB	TXT DOC RTF PDF AZW EPUB

probably the easiest part of the problem with 4 terabyte hard drives available in late 2014 for approximately £100. The biggest challenge will be choosing which format to store our data in and then devising and sticking to a plan for regularly backing it all up to secure on-site and off-site locations.

Harris (2009) argues that choosing the right digital format is crucial to avoid creating an archive that will be unreadable in 10 or 20 years' time. For text he recommends using the generic TXT format, which he claims will be readable 100 years from now, and avoid the problems faced by the BBC Domesday Project mentioned earlier. For text documents that also contain images he recommends PDF format, which is now an ISO standard, but he points out that future changes to the standard by its owner Adobe may create compatibility issues in the future. While nobody can be certain which digital formats will be readable in 100 years, it seems likely that the vast numbers of pictures currently held in JPEG format and music in MP3 format will ensure some kind of basic decoding software will be available to make sense of them. It is the less commonly used formats, particularly in the more complex area of video encoding, that may cause problems. One can imagine a new type of information professional will be required in the year 2050 who can act as a digital archaeologist and restore inaccessible photos and videos to their owners.

Putting it in the cloud

A fundamental aspect of any data backup plan is to make sure that at least one copy is kept off-site. This has been common practice for most organizations for many years and has led to the rise of facilities such as Iron Mountain, discussed earlier. There is a growing trend for private individuals to do the same, with a range of providers offering solutions for backing up personal data on off-site servers. It has been estimated that the global market for providing cloud storage services to consumers could be worth over US$16 billion by 2019 (Transparency Market Research, 2013). Technology consultant Accenture (2013) sees a growing willingness among consumers to pay for such services with a third of users happy to pay over US$10 a month. Companies offering off-site backup to consumers include Carbonite, SugarSync, Dropbox and Mozy. Typically these require software to be installed on the devices that need backing up with the backups taking place in the background while the computer is switched on. Although they offer an easy way to back up data, there are issues that need to be considered before committing to such services. One is the cost; though prices have fallen, cost is still a factor to be taken into account with Dropbox charging US$9.99 a month for 100GB and Google charging US$1.99 for the same amount of storage in its Drive service (prices correct as of August 2014). With most personal computers now having hard drives of over 500 gigabytes it is easy to see how the costs can mount up. Over a ten-year period this could add up to thousands of dollars.

Another issue is security; how can we be sure that the company we trust our data with can be relied on to keep it safe? Stories of computers and networks being hacked are common, with even large companies such as Google and Sony vulnerable to determined intruders. Finally, even if our data is secure and locked down, what happens if the company goes out of business? Will our data disappear along with the company or will we be given an opportunity to retrieve it before their servers are switched off? There are no easy answers to these questions, which many of us will have to deal with. Again, information professionals should be better placed than many to offer advice on this front as these are information management problems that organizations have faced for a number of years.

Our digital footprints

Although making sure our digital music, photos and files are preserved safely requires some careful consideration when deciding what formats and storage providers to use, once those decisions are made it is a relatively simple process of working to a system. Whatever solution is chosen will be based on the notion of backing up and storing discrete files in particular formats. Personal digital curation becomes a little more complicated when we have to deal with less tangible items of information such as e-mails, social media posts and profiles, instant messaging and other digital breadcrumbs we leave behind us as we use the web. For example, active users of Facebook build up considerable archives of posts, photos and other messages shared across their social network, which can present a valuable timeline of their lives. While we can copy our digital photos and music across different devices can we do the same with this other data? If so, how might we do so, in what format might it be, and what other services will be able to make sense of it?

Providing definitive answers to these questions is not possible as social media is still in its infancy and the policies adopted by companies such as Facebook are changing frequently. However, there has been considerable concern over the last several years that users should be able to move their data across different networks and preserve copies for posterity. For example, Google has set up an engineering team it calls the Data Liberation Front, whose aim is to make it easier for users to move their data in and out of the company's products. The group encourages anyone using a web service that holds their personal data to ask three questions before committing to the service:

• Can I get my data out in an open, interoperable, portable format?
• How much is it going to cost to get my data out?
• How much of my time is it going to take to get my data out?

In an attempt to provide positive answers to the above questions, the Data Liberation Front works with Google's product development teams to make the flow of data as smooth and as easy as possible. As part of this ambition and because of the increasing number of Google services such as Gmail, Google Plus, Picasa and so on, in 2011 the group launched a service called Google Takeout, which allows data to be taken out from multiple Google services in one click. The data is downloaded as a compressed single file, which can then be opened and ported to other compatible services. Facebook offers a similar service for a user to download a copy of their data but how easily it can then be uploaded to another social media service is uncertain. It is clearly not in Facebook's commercial interest to make it easy for its users to pack up their data and move to a competitor's site. Although a downloaded copy of a Facebook account's data might allow users to view their data offline, it is unlikely that another service would be able to make sense of the complex links with other Facebook users, which are at the heart of such a service.

Google has been at the forefront of delivering so-called 'cloud' computing services to consumers, but other companies are now also moving in to this space. In 2011 Apple announced the launch of its iCloud service, which allows users to store their music, video and other digital content in Apple's data centres. According to Sverdlik (2014), Apple's data centres now consume more energy than any other part of the business, and the company aims to generate 100% of this power from renewable sources such as solar. Also in 2011, Amazon started allowing its customers to store music and e-books bought over its service on the company's servers. Amazon's service provides off-site backup and also allows users to access their content anywhere via a web browser. While this may be a convenience for many people it presents challenges to the traditional ways we have bought and 'owned' content. These challenges are explored in other parts of this book as they have an impact on information distribution and consumption, but from a storage perspective off-site hosting begins to blur the distinction between owning a piece of content and renting it. When our music was stored on records and CDs we had legal ownership over that copy and were free to lend or sell it on to others. If our music, books and videos are stored in Amazon's, Google's or Apple's data centres then we may be restricted on how we can legally move that content around. We may be trading ownership for convenience.

So far this section has considered some of the questions we might want to consider when planning a preservation strategy for our personal data. If planned correctly the strategy should allow us to look back on our old photos, videos and e-mails in our old age and share them with our grandchildren. But what happens to that data when we are no longer here? Just as we make wills to allow the transfer of physical and monetary assets when we die should we also be making plans for others to inherit our digital legacy? Carroll and Romano (2010) think so and have written a book called *Your Digital Afterlife*, offering advice for anyone wanting to allow an orderly handover of their digital assets after their death. In the case of digital data stored on traditional media such as computer hard drives and optical discs, such a handover is relatively straightforward and can be managed as part of a traditional will, but with online data it becomes more complicated with issues of passwords and legal questions over whether social media and e-mail accounts can be transferred. Facebook has attempted to deal with this by creating 'memorialized' profiles for accounts where the owner has died. With over 1.3 billion accounts, including a rapidly growing number of users over the age of 50, this was becoming a growing issue for Facebook. By filling in a form and providing proof that the account holder has died, Facebook will freeze the pages of the deceased, not allow any more logins, and prevent the pages from showing up in searches. The comment wall will remain and be a place for friends and family to pay their respects. The pages will then act as a memorial to the deceased user or, if the relatives wish, the pages will be removed completely. It will be interesting to see how the Facebook initiative and developments across other social media platforms develop. Might such companies be legally obliged to maintain memorial sites for minimum periods or in perpetuity as they become valuable sources of the details of our everyday lives for future historians? Perhaps they will begin to take on a similar role to the National Archives in preserving our digital heritage.

The future of storage

Predicting the future of technology is generally a fool's errand but some general directions of travel can be assumed. It now seems inevitable that more of the work that has traditionally been carried out and then stored on personal computers will be managed by web or cloud services in remote locations. The increasingly pervasive nature of fixed and mobile broadband connections and the popularity of services provided by Facebook, Twitter, Google and Amazon are accelerating this process. Some of the issues around sustainable formats and security have been discussed earlier and there is still a lot of work to be done before users can be confident that services are secure and will not lock them in. Organizations are already grappling with these questions and increasingly it will also be a problem for individuals.

One of the defining characteristics of the computing revolution has been a steady increase in the power of devices and a corresponding fall in their cost to users, which in the context of microprocessors has been referred to as Moore's law. Data storage is no exception: Komorowski (2014) calculates that the retail price of computer hard drives fell from approximately US$9 per gigabyte in 2000 to 3 cents per gigabyte in 2014, a decrease of more than 99%. Projecting that decrease forward to 2020 would result in 1 terabyte drives costing less than a dollar. Data storage is being commoditized and its cost will become negligible, but the services around storage such as accessibility and security will command a price premium.

The price example mentioned above uses traditional hard drives comprising spinning magnetic platters to show the fall in prices, but just as floppy discs are rarely used now, so those types of disc will probably not be in a personal computer bought in 2020. Solid state drives and flash memory cards are the norm in smart phones, tablet computers and most music players, and are also appearing in laptops and personal computers. Although they are currently more expensive to produce than traditional hard drives, their speed, size, power consumption and lack of moving parts make them attractive for portable device manufacturers. Sales of traditional drives have been falling in recent years and Samsung's sale of its hard drive manufacturing unit in

2011 to Seagate is an indicator that the market is changing to favour new technologies.

One of the biggest challenges for producers of data storage technologies will be to cope with the competing demands for increased storage capacities but at lower prices and with decreased physical footprints and energy consumption but faster access and write speeds. Reducing the energy requirements of data centres is a growing concern for many of the larger internet companies as we saw earlier, with Apple turning to renewable sources to meet its power needs. Much of the energy consumed is used to cool the many thousands of computer servers housed in such centres, which according to Fehrenbacher (2011) has led Google and Facebook to build centres in Scandinavia to make use of the natural air cooling that the cold winter climate allows. It is a sign that companies are increasingly working with nature to build sustainable businesses rather than consuming ever-increasing amounts of energy to counter the by-products of large-scale computing. As global warming becomes a higher priority for all of us and cloud computing replaces the traditional personal computer perhaps we will see a migration of computing facilities to the colder northern hemisphere. Radical new techniques for increasing storage capacities are also being explored with holographic discs and even protein-based DVDs under development. Herrman and Buchanan (2010) discuss the possibility of manipulating the DNA of bacteria as a solution, claiming that 'up to 100 bits of data can be attached to each organism. Scientists successfully encoded and attached the phrase "e=mc2 1905" to the DNA of bacillus subtilis, a common soil bacteria.' In 2012 Ewan Birney, associate director of the European Bioinformatics Institute, announced he had been able to store all 154 of Shakespeare's sonnets and other data using DNA molecules (Purcell, 2013). In the short to medium term we will have to rely on tried and tested storage technologies such as hard drives and solid state drives, but the laws of physics may render them obsolete in 10 or 20 years and holograms and bacteria may be the solution to preserving our digital heritage.

Concluding comments

While the amount of information we are creating and storing has never been so large, it has also never been so vulnerable to loss and destruction. Besides the media it is stored on, digital data cannot be seen, and the old saying 'out of sight, out of mind' seems increasingly relevant in this context. Organizations with a legal and commercial interest in preserving data will continue to develop new and innovative ways of doing this but what about the rest of us? When a lifetime's photos, videos and e-mails can be lost as our computer hard drive finally expires, personal information storage solutions will become ever more relevant. Information preservation and collection management policies may no longer be the sole preserve of the information professional.

4

New models of information distribution

Introduction

At the heart of the current information revolution are radical changes to the way information, in all its forms, is distributed. Obviously, the internet has been a key driver of these changes, but so too have other advances and investments in communication networks, particularly on the mobile front. By the beginning of 2015 almost one-half (approximately 3 billion people) of the world's population were connected to the internet while more than 90% of the world had mobile phones; much of the information we consume is carried across these networks. Broadly, we are moving from a centralized broadcast model of information distribution to a more distributed and, some would argue, more democratic model, where many of the established information gatekeepers are being bypassed. Just as the railways in the 19th century transformed the movement of goods and people across many western economies, communication systems are doing the same for information. However, a key difference between these networks is the ease of access with which individuals and organizations can access them; another is the fundamental difference between the physical world and the digital. Systems for moving objects such as roads and railways are limited in their capacity to carry people and vehicles, as anyone who has to travel in rush hour knows; digital networks, particularly those using optical fibre, are far less constrained. This chapter explains some of the key technical characteristics of our communication networks within the context of the radical changes that are taking place in the information sector. The competing interests of information producers and network operators are explored and the implications for information professionals considered.

The architecture of the internet

To appreciate the significance of the changes that are taking place in the world of information it is important to understand how the internet works, at a basic level at least. While anyone who has grown up in the last 20 years, the so-called 'digital natives', may take an internet connection for granted it is worth looking back at where this network came from and how it evolved. The significance of this will become clearer when we consider some of the threats to the open nature and what Zittrain (2008) calls the 'generative' nature of the internet. This will be examined at the end of this chapter but first let us look back a few years to when the internet was born.

According to Leiner at al. (2009), the origins of the internet can be traced back to the early 1960s when a researcher at MIT proposed an idea for what he called a 'galactic network' that would comprise a globally distributed set of connected computers. At the same time another MIT researcher published a paper outlining a new method for transporting data across communication networks, called packet switching. The key difference between packet switching and the traditional circuit switching method was that messages were broken down into data packets and could be distributed across a network using multiple connections to be reassembled at the other end into the original message. This was a far more efficient way of moving data and was also more resilient to network faults as packets that did not arrive at the final destination could be sent for again. With a traditional circuit switching method a single connection was required between the sender and the receiver, which slowed down networks, and if a problem occurred then the entire message needed to be sent again. Packet switching allowed networks to carry far more data and at lower cost to those sending and receiving messages. Throughout the 1960s, researchers in the USA and UK explored the potential of packet switching and by 1969 ARPANET, the forerunner of the internet, carried its first message between Stanford University and University of California, Los Angeles. The network was expanded over the 1970s and systems and standards were agreed that allowed services such as e-mail and file transport to be added. These standards or protocols are a key factor in explaining why the internet has evolved to its present state. As Leiner et al. (2009, 24) explain: 'The Internet as we know it embodies a key underlying technical idea, namely that of open architecture networking. In this approach, the choice of any individual network technology was not dictated by a particular network architecture but rather could be selected freely by a provider and made to interwork with the other networks through a meta-level "Internetworking Architecture".'

Just as any vehicle that is built within certain size parameters can use our road networks, so any computer that complied with freely available protocols could connect to the internet. The internet was developed by researchers who wanted to create a network that would allow the greatest number of people to access it and this was achieved through the creation of and compliance to open standards. The non-profit nature of their endeavours lies at the heart of their creation and is a good example of the role that public bodies can play, albeit often unwittingly, in the development of major innovations.

While the internet continued to grow throughout the 1980s and into the early 1990s it was largely used by the academic community to share information and there was little commercial activity taking place on or around it. Outside universities it was expensive and technically complicated for individuals or organizations to connect to the network with hardware, software and connection charges running into the thousands of dollars. At this time other private networks started to emerge that offered users access to a range of information and communication services. These included CompuServe, Delphi and America Online (AOL) and were designed to offer a limited range of proprietary and sometimes third party information services such as news, discussion forums and early versions of electronic mail. One of the limitations of such networks was their 'walled garden' approach to service provision where subscribers were limited to offerings vetted by the provider. From a commercial perspective this control has a certain logic: why go to the expense of building a network across which anyone can deliver services that could compete with the network owner's offerings? Controlling what is offered over the network allows the owner to take a greater share of the revenues that flow over it. The downside for users to such an arrangement is a restriction of choice and the stifling of innovation, as well as limitations as to what can be done on the network. Sending e-mails between CompuServe subscribers was fine but the problems arose when you wanted to send an e-mail to someone on another network as they were not designed to be interoperable.

Similar networks were experimented with by some of the large cable television operators in the USA at this time where the notion of interactive television looked like becoming a reality. Unlike traditional terrestrial television broadcast networks, cable television networks had wires going into subscribers' homes, which could be used for both sending information down to households and receiving an upstream from them. A two-way stream could allow customers to request information services such as the delivery of videos on demand and online banking, and the ordering of physical items such as pizzas and groceries. One of the largest interactive television trials took place in Orlando, Florida, in the mid-1990s where Time Warner invested over US$100 million in providing set top boxes and upgraded network connections to thousands of subscribers. However, the high infrastructure costs and the lack of enthusiasm among subscribers for the more expensive services offered led to its cancellation in 1997.

One of the fundamental issues that users of online networks such as CompuServe and interactive cable television networks such as Time Warner's faced was lack of choice. The services they offered were dictated by the network owners so pizzas could only be ordered from one company that had tied up an exclusive deal with Time Warner or news was provided by a CompuServe-approved supplier. This bore little resemblance to the high street or the shopping mall where competing shops and banks are free to ply their wares and customers can choose based on price, quality and level of service provision. Ultimately, this is one of the key reasons for the failure of such networks to survive once the internet began to open up to end-users outside universities. It was the development in the 1990s of the world wide web as a graphical interface, sitting on top of the internet as an open distribution network, that provided users and information service providers with the incentive they needed to move to this 'new' environment, which had quietly been growing since the 1970s. Isenberg (1998) refers to the internet as the 'stupid network' in ironic reference to the so-called 'intelligent networks' that were being promoted by the major telecommunication networks. The ability of these operators to offer services such as caller ID and call transfer relied on centralized computer switching within the network and relatively simple telephone devices at the consumer end. Isenberg's 'stupid network' was only concerned with moving digital bits from sender to receiver and left it up to the computing devices at either end to make sense of them. This new model of information distribution threatened the control that network operators had traditionally exercised and put the users in a position of power for the first time.

By the mid-1990s it was becoming clear to many that the 'open' internet had a more promising future than the closed networks described above, as it allowed anyone who was using the right equipment to connect with each other. E-mail took on a new lease of life as it was no longer controlled by commercially motivated organizations and became the internet's first 'killer application'. The world wide web then allowed more than just text-based information to be presented to users, with a website becoming as indispensable to organizations as having a telephone or fax number. The launch of the Mosaic web browser in 1993 along with the rise of e-mail as a communications tool brought the internet into the mainstream, and by 1995 there were an estimated 16 million users worldwide. Within three years this had grown to almost 150 million and by the end of 2000 there were 360 million global users. At the same time the cost to users of connecting to the internet fell, as did the computing hardware, but connection speeds increased. In 1995 the typical domestic download speed was 14.4 kilobits per second, which restricted the types of data that could be downloaded to text and low resolution graphics. Gradually the speed of modems increased but it was not until the introduction of broadband connections either using the asymmetric digital subscriber line (ADSL) technologies of the telephone companies or high-speed cable television connections that higher bandwidth services such as telephony or video streaming were possible.

When it became clear that the internet was more than a fad like CB Radio had been in the 1970s, the financial community began to take an interest and by the late 1990s the first internet boom had begun. Telecom operators invested millions in upgrading their networks and laying fibre optic cables across most of the developed world. New entrants such as Global Crossing and Level 3 Communications raised hundreds of millions of dollars on the capital markets to build out entirely new fibre networks in anticipation of the rapidly growing demand for bandwidth. It resembled the building of the railway networks in the UK and USA in the mid-19th century when speculators raised money from investors to fund what they saw as the future of transportation. Unfortunately, for many of these investors the result was the same: the networks were built but the financial returns were not as expected and fortunes were lost. Global Crossing, for example, had built a high-speed data network spanning 27 countries by 2002 but as bandwidth prices fell due to over-capacity the company declared bankruptcy in that year with debts of over US$12 billion. However, as with the railways, what was bad news for investors was ultimately good news for internet users as the legacy of companies like Global Crossing was a backbone network fit for the 21st century. The dotcom bust of 2000 may have cleared out a number of weak companies built on flimsy business models but it paved the way for the second generation of internet companies commonly referred to as Web 2.0.

Distribution and disintermediation

We have seen how the internet has developed from humble beginnings in university research centres and how it has emerged as a key network for distributing information. This section considers the impact it is having on a range of information-intensive industries and the information professionals that rely on the internet as a distribution network. In Chapter 2 we saw how new technologies are leading to the creation of new types of information and in this chapter we will explore how those technologies are changing the way information is carried from creators to end-users and, in many instances, leading to the disintermediation of traditional gatekeepers, including information professionals. Disintermediation is the bypassing of established players in a value chain either through the introduction of new technologies or via new business processes. In the physical world the growth of farm shops can be seen as an attempt by farmers to disintermediate wholesale and retailers and sell their produce directly to consumers. Although this has not checked the growth of large supermarkets, such ventures along with farmers' markets allow the original producers of our food to keep a larger share of the profits. In Chapter 2 we saw how bloggers were attempting to do something similar in their attempts to bypass traditional publishing models. If you are a producer of information then the internet presents an obvious channel to get your content directly to your customers without having to go through intermediaries, which would want to take their share of profits out of the value chain, but the theoretical prospects for information distribution promised by the internet do not always work in practice. In a number of instances we are seeing new intermediaries such as Amazon, iTunes and eBay dislodging established players from the physical world but still acting as gatekeepers between buyers and sellers.

In the information world the internet has been a disruptive force for providers of information services and the information professionals who buy them. Perhaps the most obvious impact has been on the information that has relied on paper as its distribution method, with directories and encyclopedias suffering the most. However, it should be remembered that digital online information services predate the world wide web by almost 20 years. In 1972 the Lockheed Corporation offered online access to its Dialog set of databases for a fee, starting an industry of commercial online information access that continues into the 21st century. Owners of databases and information products realized there was a potential to sell their assets through hosts such as Dialog, DataStar and Orbit to interested parties. Purchasers tended to be librarians and information professionals who were often the only people trained to interrogate such databases. Proper training was important as the hosts were difficult to search, with each having their own search languages and syntax. The databases were also expensive to access, typically charging a usage fee depending on the time spent on the service and the amount of data downloaded. The data access fees charged by the local telecommunications operator and the modem and terminal hardware also added to the cost. These financial and technical barriers restricted who could access the service as inefficient searching could result in substantial costs to the person requiring the information. According to Williams (2005), there were 4018 online databases on offer by 1990, with the vast majority only accessible through hosts such as Dialog. Several thousand databases were also accessible via other media such as CD-ROM, diskette and magnetic tape but throughout the 1990s these declined in significance as online access became the norm. By 2004 the number of online databases had grown to 9489 but Williams (2005) points out that by then their growth had slowed.

Two of the key changes for database providers that have taken place since the late 1990s are a move to using the internet as their platform for delivery, and the web as the interface for users to search for information. While some of the large database hosts still allow users to search using their proprietary command languages they have also introduced simplified searching making the experience closer to an internet search engine, and experimented with different charging methods in an attempt to encourage more casual searchers to try their services. This has been met with mixed and often disappointing responses as many information seekers do not expect to pay for information accessed over the internet and are often satisfied with free sources. The struggles by large information vendors such as Thomson, Dow Jones and Reuters to adapt to this new world of 'free' information can be seen in the corporate mergers and joint ventures that have taken place over the previous 15 years but which have yet to find a business model that will attract non-information professionals to pay for information. We saw in Chapter 2 that some newspaper providers are having moderate success at charging their readers for online access. At the core of this problem for vendors is the much used and often misunderstood phrase, 'Information wants to be free.' This is attributed to Stewart Brand, who according to Clarke (2000) said at a hacker conference in 1984: 'On the one hand information wants to be expensive, because it's so valuable. The right information in the right place just changes your life. On the other hand, information wants to be free, because the cost of getting it out is getting lower and lower all the time. So you have these two fighting against each other.'

CASE STUDY DataSift

DataSift was founded in 2010 in Reading, UK, and offers its customers access to billions of posts from a range of social media platforms including Twitter, Facebook and YouTube. The company has developed sophisticated algorithms and data processing capabilities to search through social media data and make sense of the information they contain. The company claims, 'Our vision is that all organizations will make the use of Social Data integral to their planning and decision-making processes.' Typically, clients use DataSift's services to understand the sentiment of social media posts, whether people are making positive or negative comments about them, and to try to gauge public opinion on a range of issues. The company is one of the few to have full access to Twitter's so-called 'firehose of data', so it can analyse over 300 million tweets every day and posts from other social platforms. As more data, personal and business, is distributed across social networks, services such as those provided by DataSift will become more central to the information requirements of organizations in the same way that third party information aggregators such as Dialog have been for the last 30 years. In an age where many information resources are becoming commoditized and information aggregators are struggling to justify their fees, companies like DataSift can determine contextualized meaning from information flows that are in demand.

The internet is now a highly efficient distribution network for exchanging information and is forcing information providers to re-evaluate their business models (see case study on DataSift above). When information was scarce and difficult to access it was possible to charge a premium for it but when information that is perceived to be 'good enough' is easily available at no cost then the equation changes. This is also having an impact on information professionals, who have traditionally been the gatekeepers to online databases. The advent of desktop computers, the internet and then search engines such as Google has, for many people, bypassed the need to go to a librarian.

The new intermediaries

It is the intrinsic nature of information and, in particular, the characteristics of digital information, that gives credence to the notion that information may want to be free. Shapiro and Varian (1999) explain the concept of 'first-copy costs' whereby the cost of an information product such as a book or a film is sunk into the cost of producing the first copy. Once that first book is published then the subsequent copies comprise only the marginal cost of printing. Shapiro and Varian's seminal work on the internet and its impact on information producers leads them to comment: 'Information delivered over a network in digital form exhibits the first-copy problem in an extreme way: once the first copy of the information has been produced, additional copies cost essentially nothing' (Shapiro and Varian, 1999, 21).

Combining these characteristics with the non-rivalrous nature of digital information presents challenges to anyone hoping to make money from its sale. Non-rivalry is an economic term referring to commodities such as information whose consumption by one person does not prohibit their consumption by another. For example, a newspaper is not destroyed by being read, whereas a cake can only be eaten once. Digital information suffers even less from rivalry in that multiple digital copies can be read at once whereas an analogue equivalent such as a book can only be read by one person at a time.

Intermediaries in the shadows

One of the sectors impacted the most by the rise of the internet has been the music industry. The popularity of the CD format for music throughout the 1980s and 1990s meant that when the internet started to become popular among consumers, most young people already had digital collections of music that could relatively easily be ripped from CDs to computer hard drives. The MP3 compression format for audio files made it possible for large music collections to be shrunk to one-tenth of the storage space size they required. Smaller file sizes were also easier to send over the internet, an important factor when most people still relied on slow dial-up connections. These developments conspired in the late 1990s to create an environment where a 19-year-old university student called Shawn Fanning created and launched an internet-based music sharing system called Napster, which within a year had amassed 20 million users who were sharing 80 million songs. Napster was a great success at creating a vibrant and popular service but its disregard for US copyright law brought it to the attention of the music industry, and in 2001, after a series of legal battles in the courts, the service was shut down.

In some ways the Napster story remains a footnote in the history of the internet as the company lasted little more than a year and never managed to develop a profitable and, more importantly, legal business model. The story highlights the disruptive nature of the internet as a distribution system for digital information and the threat it poses to established industries. Knopper quotes Kearby, founder of an online music service, describing his experience of dealing with music industry executives in the late 1990s: 'Some of them were more interested in experimenting than others, there's no doubt about it. But they were, in effect, buggy-whip manufacturers, trying to keep the auto at bay as long as they could' (Knopper, 2009, 120).

Napster was followed by similar initiatives such as LimeWire and Kazaa, which made use of peer-to-peer technologies to allow users to share sections of their computer hard drives primarily for the purpose of sharing music and increasingly for video files. Video compression protocols were allowing movies to be compressed into smaller files in the same way that the MP3 format had done for music. LimeWire and Kazaa met with similar legal objections from the music industry as Napster and they were eventually forced to prevent their users from trading copyright-infringing materials. More recently, The Pirate Bay has been the centre of attention from the music and film industries but aggressive legal action from the film and music industries and the jailing of one of its founders, Peter Sunde, in 2014 have had a significant impact on its operations. Many ISPs around the world now block access to The Pirate Bay, which makes it inaccessible to people unless they know how to circumvent the block. The Pirate Bay and other similar services typically use bittorrent technology, which is an efficient way of distributing digital files across the internet using peer-to-peer principles. It works most effectively for popular files, as separate sections of a file are downloaded simultaneously from multiple computers on the peer-to-peer network. This reduces the bandwidth strain on any individual computer's network connection and spreads the load across the internet. The historic popularity of bittorrent sites such as The Pirate Bay, Torrentz and IsoHunt among file shares can be seen by examining global internet traffic patterns. In 2008, bittorrent traffic accounted for over 30% of all internet traffic in the USA and Europe (Sandvine, 2014), but by 2014 these figures had fallen to 6% in the USA and 15% in Europe, possibly signalling the beginning of the demise of illegal file sharing among the masses. It is worth noting that online piracy outside much of the USA and Europe is still rampant with the music and film sectors finding it difficult to have any impact on copyright infringement. There is considerable debate about the impact on legitimate media sales of online piracy. Being able to determine accurately a causal link between illegal file downloads and a decline in the sales of CDs and DVDs is not possible as a number of other factors need to be taken into account. The next section considers legitimate attempts to use the internet as a distribution tool; although favoured by many in the music industry, these are still bypassing traditional intermediaries such as retail and rental stores.

Copyright-friendly intermediaries

The launch of the iTunes online music store in 2003 marked the beginning of a serious fight back by the music industry to sell music over the internet. Created by Apple Computer, Inc., as a way to allow its iPod customers to buy music online, the initiative was a great success and in early 2010 announced its ten-billionth song download. Competitors have emerged since 2003 but, with the exception of Amazon's music download service launched in 2008, none have come close to replicating the success of iTunes as a download service.

Music streaming services such as Pandora, Last.fm and Spotify have also gained in popularity and possibly present a transition away from buying and 'owning' music to a rental model. The recent decline in the sales of music via iTunes is a strong signal that streaming music and video services may be the future for the media sector. This is more akin to the broadcast model we are familiar with, such as radio and television, but offers consumers the advantage of more choice over what is played. However, the impact on intermediaries in the value chain such as shops is the same, and the impact on the content creators, the musicians, may also be considerable. While streaming services, particularly those such as Pandora and Spotify that offer recommendations, may help emerging artists break through to the mainstream there are financial implications as well. According to McCandless (2010), for musicians to earn the US monthly minimum wage of US$1160, they would need to sell 143 self-pressed CDs at US$9.99 a unit, 1161 CDs via a music retailer, 1229 album downloads via iTunes or just over 4 million plays on Spotify. McCandless acknowledges that these figures are based on assumptions about the royalty deal a musician will have made with a record company but they illustrate the difficulties of making money in this new environment. However, once a new technology becomes favoured by consumers it is virtually impossible to persuade those consumers to revert back to an old one. Manufacturers of VCR players, audio cassettes and transistor radios will testify to that. We are now seeing similar developments in the book publishing industry, as sales of e-book readers, particularly the Amazon Kindle, took off in 2011 alongside the demise of many bookshops, including more than 500 operated by Borders, which went into liquidation in the same year.

Online video – we are all celebrities now

We have seen how the music industry has been disrupted by the internet as an alternative distribution network for its content. Something similar is also occurring in the distribution of video content as Hollywood and the television broadcast companies struggle to cope with viewers seeking their entertainment from alternative providers such as YouTube and BitTorrent. Whereas in the past you needed complex distribution agreements with cinema or broadcast network owners for your films and programmes to be seen by a mass audience, there is a ready audience of almost 3 billion internet users freely accessible to view your masterpiece. YouTube celebrities such as Justin Bieber and Rebecca Black have used this free video network to attract millions of fans and secure lucrative contracts with more mainstream media companies. Amateur musician Rebecca Black's Friday music video was viewed almost 170 million times in its first three months on YouTube in 2011, while the popularity of Justin Bieber's home-made pop videos brought him to the attention of the music industry.

Although these high-profile examples are exceptions, with most amateur videos never receiving more than a few hundred viewings, it is the scale of YouTube as a video distribution network that is most worthy of attention. Founded in 2005 by three young entrepreneurs, it was bought 18 months later by Google for US$1.65 billion and since then has become the dominant online space for posting and viewing video. By August 2014 over 100 hours of video were being uploaded to the service every minute with 6 billion hours of its videos watched each month (YouTube, 2014). One of the key reasons for its success is the ease with which videos can be uploaded at no cost to the uploader or viewer. Another important factor is how YouTube makes it easy for people to share videos across the internet by allowing videos to be embedded within other websites. Rather than expecting everyone to visit the YouTube website to view video content, the company offers a unique embed code that can be pasted into other sites. Although this may reduce the number of visitors to its own site, it capitalizes on the viral nature of some internet content by encouraging its propagation across other websites.

In this way YouTube is making the most of two features of the internet that distinguishes it from traditional broadcast media networks. First, it is building its service on an open distribution network that treats video data streams the same as any other internet traffic and allows anyone with an internet connection to upload and view video content. Second, it is leveraging open web standards to allow video content to be freely shared across other people's and companies' websites, a bold point of difference from most media organizations, which seek to control how their content is consumed. While most people still view video content through their television there are signs that YouTube is moving into becoming more of a distribution service for mainstream content and live events. In 2012 over 8 million people watched Felix Baumgartner's record breaking 128,000 foot skydive live via YouTube, marking a significant move into competing directly with broadcast media networks. The similarities with broadcast television networks continue with the development of YouTube channels, which allow video producers to have their own area on YouTube to showcase their content. Some of these channels have audiences that many traditional television networks would be proud of. Barcroft Media, for example, has more than half a million subscribers (as of August 2014) to its channel and received over 500 million views for its short factual videos, which range from, 'Rescue dog kisses cute cheetah' to 'Giant Amazon model dwarfs men for a living'. Whether there is a sustainable business in producing these two or three-minute films, often based on sensational or trivial subjects is debatable, but the fact that the company employs 20 full-time producers (Dredge, 2014) shows there is a market for bit-sized video content in the short term at least.

Another sign that YouTube is maturing into a broad multimedia platform is the company's offering of pay-per-view film rentals putting it into competition with video streaming services such as Netflix (see case study opposite) and Amazon Instant Video. In the same way that music is increasingly distributed as a streamed service, so too video is moving from disc to the internet. These changes were summed up in 2014 by the head of The New York Times Company and former director-general of the BBC Mark Thompson, when he launched the newspaper group's 14 channel internet video offering. Acknowledging that technology has made it possible for a newspaper to move into video content he said, 'The internet is the great leveller... Video used to be the sole preserve of broadcasters' (Economist, 2014). While print publishers may be moving into creating and distributing video content it is perhaps a sign of where the media is heading in that no video or broadcast organizations are moving into the newspaper business.

CASE STUDY NETFLIX

Netflix was established in 1997 in the USA and for its first ten years was a DVD delivery service, which allowed customers to order the DVDs they wanted via the Netflix website. These were then delivered via the postal service with new DVDs despatched when the customer returned the watched ones via prepaid envelopes. This hybrid business model which combined the virtuality of the internet with the physicality of DVDs and the postal service was a great success. In 2007 the company began delivering video content via the internet, which coincided with a decline in the popularity of DVDs. Most of the revenues now come from subscriptions to the video on-demand service, which allows customers unlimited viewing of any of the thousands of films and television series it hosts. The popularity of this service, particularly in the USA, is marked by more than 50 million users paying monthly subscriptions to the company with some estimates suggesting that it accounts for almost a third of all internet traffic at peak watching times. In 2013, reinforcing the adage that 'content is king', Netflix aired the series *House of Cards*, which it had spent approximately US$100 million producing. The success of this series and others it has financed signal that acting as only an intermediary in the internet age may not be a sustainable business model. Owning the intellectual property which flows across the internet pipes and the delivery service appears to be a more attractive proposition, providing it is priced at a level that reduces the incentive for online piracy.

The video classroom

The longer-term impact that the internet and YouTube in particular will have on established distribution networks for video content will take a number of years to become apparent. On a smaller scale many organizations are making use of the service to offer educational video content to end-users. Universities are increasingly uploading videos of lectures, allowing anyone anywhere in the world to view world-leading academics talk about their specialist subject areas. In the USA, the MIT has been an active user of YouTube since 2005 and by late 2014 had uploaded almost 3000 videos, which had received over 70 million views, with its dedicated channel having more than 500,000 subscribers. The videos that MIT uploads are primarily recordings of formal lectures, opening up one of the world's leading universities to a global audience. While these recordings will never attract the audience numbers that Justin Bieber and Rebecca Black enjoy, it might reasonably be argued that their impact on learning and development will be significantly higher.

Even more ambitious in its attempt to open up learning to those wishing to improve their education is the Khan Academy, discussed in the case study opposite. The common link between the Khan Academy and those universities uploading their lectures to YouTube and other online platforms is a belief that education does not need to be restricted to the classroom and lecture theatre. The internet presents a supplementary and possibly even, some would argue, an alternative to mainstream education. Apple Computer's iTunes U is an embodiment of this as it brings together its iTunes online library as a distribution service with the educational content of many of the world's leading universities. Although iTunes U is perhaps less open than the open web as a platform for distribution, as it requires the use of iTunes software and devices such as the iPod which can run the software, it is an important development in the spread of online learning. Once the appropriate software and hardware are in place it is free to use and allows users to download more than 750,000 lectures, audio and video, from more than 1200 universities including Oxford University and the Open University in the UK and Stanford and Yale universities in the USA. In many cases the multimedia content is supplemented by PDF and EPUB format materials.

However, it is important to remember that a university education involves more than simply attending lectures, making notes and sitting exams. Much of the learning takes place in the seminars and tutorials where concepts are discussed and students are encouraged to explore ideas, explain opposing arguments and develop the crucial skill of critical thinking. Writing about the power of technology to transform established industries and organizational practices, Jarvis (2009) acknowledges the limitations of online learning and explains that while it may be useful to develop a specific skill, such as how to learn video editing or speak French, it can never replace a good teacher for more complex endeavours such as understanding the principles of thermodynamics, the philosophy of science or heart surgery. However, Jarvis does believe services like iTunes and YouTube have the potential to alter the way universities will work in the future. He argues, 'Universities need to ask what value they add in educational transactions. We need to ask when and why it is necessary to be in the same room with fellow students and instructors. Classroom time is valuable but not always necessary' (Jarvis, 2009, 216).

Perhaps a natural evolution of online distance learning has been the rise of so-called massive open online courses (MOOCs). MOOCs typically make use of online video and digital resources to deliver lectures and online quizzes and tests. Work submitted by students on MOOCs is typically either assessed by fellow students or automatically by the software used to deliver the course. The massive class sizes of some MOOCs rules out traditional marking by tutors, particularly when most of the courses are offered at no cost to the students. A number of universities have developed or spun out their own MOOC software including edX, Coursera and Udacity. The initial popularity of the MOOC concept was fuelled by the large numbers of students enrolling on courses with some attracting tens of thousands of students for individual courses. Many traditional universities became concerned that their student numbers would drop as the incentive to pay ever-increasing fees to attend a physical campus would drop off in a world where MIT and Stanford were offering MOOCs delivered by some of their leading academics. As with many potentially disruptive technologies, some of these concerns were misplaced and the extremely high non-completion rate for many courses delivered this way highlighted weaknesses in this model of delivery. But the MOOC is unlikely to disappear and for some types of courses and students there is undoubtedly a place for this innovation. A number of universities see it as a complementary technology, which can enrich the learning experience of students enrolled on traditional campuses.

Perhaps when education is freed from the classroom, and where appropriate makes use of new distribution platforms, the way we think about schools and universities will change. Moving from an age of scarcity where class sizes were limited by physical spaces to one where a lecture can be seen by millions of people and reviewed as many times as required by those struggling to understand difficult concepts will require different thinking on the part of those managing our educational establishments. For some this will be disruptive as it will require new ways of working and learning but, as businesses are finding across many sectors, when information finds new ways of flowing to those who need it there is little that can be done to stop it.

CASE STUDY THE KHAN ACADEMY

Established in 2006 by Salman Khan, the Khan Academy operates as a not-for-profit educational organization, which offers free access to over 33,000 video lectures and tutorials, primarily on scientific and technical subjects. Salman Khan started the Academy after receiving positive feedback from viewers of short videos he had posted to YouTube to help his cousin with his mathematics homework. Since then he has received funding from Google and the Bill and Melinda Gates Foundation, which has enabled the tutorials to become more sophisticated with users able to complete interactive lessons at their own pace. Users are able to access the service at home, and teachers can integrate Khan Academy lessons into their teaching and monitor the progress of students as they work through the online lessons. The Khan Academy YouTube channel had by late 2014 received more than 470 million views and had over 2 million subscribers. While online educational resources have been in use since the beginning of the web, what makes this initiative unique is the volume of materials it contains, its interactive features that work with classroom teaching and, perhaps most important, that it is free. The Khan Academy's mission is to 'provide a world-class education to anyone, anywhere' (www.khanacademy.org/about). In a similar way to the iTunes U initiative, it is taking advantage of an open and easy to access network to overcome the traditional model of education delivery based on the principles of scarcity.

Internet entrepreneur Jeff Dachis's comment in the 1990s that 'everything that can be digital, will be' (Dishman, 2011) seems increasingly prescient and one that information professionals cannot ignore as they plan their careers over the coming decade. Many creators of information, whether for educational, business or entertainment purposes, have seen their value chains disrupted and in many cases made less profitable. Intermediaries further down the chain have also suffered as the new distribution networks for digital content have bypassed them entirely. The following section explores the impact these changes are having on the public sector and, in particular, how our governments communicate with us.

Open government and the internet

The notion of open government refers to the perceived right of citizens to have access to information about the workings of government and the decisions that are made in the process of governance at local and national levels. Increasingly, the principles of open government are becoming enshrined in legislation, such as freedom of information laws, which places obligations on public sector bodies to release certain types of information when requested. Although some countries such as the UK, Japan and Germany have only enacted such legislation since 2000, others have been more progressive, with Sweden adopting aspects of open government in its constitution in the late 18th century. The principles of open government lie at the heart of any democracy with the belief that for citizens to make informed decisions about who should govern them, free access to relevant information about issues of state is required. It is hard to hold politicians and civil servants to account at the ballot box for their actions if we do not know what they have been doing while in office. There are obvious exceptions to this accountability when it comes to issues of national security and law enforcement.

Proactive government

Legislation relating to freedom of information and the obligations such laws put on public bodies is a natural focus for anyone interested in open government. However, information technologies, in particular the internet, have probably had a similar impact in opening up the workings of government. Traditionally, information from government and public bodies has been mediated by journalists, whether through the work of investigative assignments, party political broadcasts or interviews. The media still plays an important role in holding politicians and public servants to account but the internet has provided a direct channel through which public bodies can communicate with citizens. This was possible in the pre-internet era through the use of government advertising campaigns on public interest matters such as health, safe driving and crime issues where billboards, newspaper advertisements and leaflets would be deployed to get messages across. These techniques are still used, but they are expensive and not always effective in reaching the people who want or need the information. Dissemination via websites is becoming increasingly important as a method for making public information easily available. Research in the UK by the Central Office of Information (COI, 2011) underlines this and shows that the 37 websites managed by British central government departments attracted 1.3 billion visits between April 2010 and March 2011. However, despite the efficiency of the internet as a distribution network, maintaining those 37 sites required significant investment with £148.9 million spent over the year on staff and other costs. Although the costs of maintaining that web presence are substantial the cost of pushing out that volume of information using traditional methods such as advertising and leaflets would be considerably higher.

The benefits of more proactive public websites were recognized in 1998 when the UK-based Campaign for Freedom of Information (CFoI) presented an award to the inquiry into the disease bovine spongiform encephalopathy (BSE) for its website. The BSE Inquiry had been set up in 1998 to investigate the spread among cattle of the disease, commonly called mad cow disease, and its spread to humans. The inquiry took place in an atmosphere of mistrust among the British public who felt they had been misled by the government over the dangers posed by eating meat from infected cattle. The CFoI applauded the openness of the inquiry and the documentation it made available via its website. Evidence for witness statements was uploaded to the site within hours of it being taken, allowing interested parties to see at first-hand what was being said rather than relying solely on media reporting or printed transcripts that were normally charged for. According to the CFoI (1998), in the first six weeks of the inquiry, some 7500 witness statements had been downloaded and 14,000 copies of transcripts had been downloaded by visitors from 64 countries.

Defensive government

Across most developed countries the internet has been used by public bodies to make information more accessible to citizens, which most would argue was a positive development in strengthening the democratic process. However, the proactive pushing of information out by government through its own websites can be contrasted with the publishing of information by third parties, which may not be so welcome by those in power. One of the key functions of journalists has been to expose wrongdoing by those in power but the internet is allowing others to join in this process. The WikiLeaks website is a good example of how the internet can circumvent traditional communication channels in a similar way that Napster did with the music industry. Set up in 2006 and fronted by Julian Assange, the WikiLeaks site claims to be:

> a not-for-profit media organisation. Our goal is to bring important news and information to the public. We provide an innovative, secure and anonymous way for sources to leak information to our journalists (our electronic drop box). One of our most important activities is to publish original source material alongside our news stories so readers and historians alike can see evidence of the truth.
>
> (WikiLeaks, n.d.)

WikiLeaks has certainly been successful in providing information to journalists and been at the centre of a number of high-profile stories relating to the Iraq war, prisoner detentions in Guantanamo Bay, confidential diplomatic cables and others. In many respects the site is simply carrying on a long tradition of helping the media publish stories based on leaked, confidential information, but it is the scale of the operation and the open publishing of the leaked information on its website that has caught the attention of governments, security services and the media. The site offers links to millions of downloadable files with hundreds of thousands relating to the Iraq war alone that had been classified as confidential by the US military.

Despite attempts, some temporarily successful, by public bodies around the world to shut the WikiLeaks site down, it has managed to maintain a web presence. This is partly because of the determination of its backers, but also a result of the nature of the internet itself, with the hosting of the site moving between and across countries making it less vulnerable to legal or technical attempts to close it down. Whether WikiLeaks will survive in the longer term remains to be seen but it seems unlikely that under the current structure and governance of the internet we will return to the more restricted information distribution model that existed before 2006. The constant demand by the media and much of the general public for greater openness by public bodies and the growth in technologies that facilitate this will ensure that governments will find it harder, if not impossible, to turn back the clock.

Offensive government

One of the most high-profile displays of government leaks has been the documents released into the public domain by the former Central Intelligence Agency security analyst Edward Snowden. In some respects the information leaked by Snowden is a natural evolution of the WikiLeaks phenomena and a sign that governments are finding it increasingly difficult to keep secrets in the digital age, but it is the information contained in Snowden's documents which has been of concern to many internet observers. They reveal the extent to which the US, UK and Australian secret services have been intercepting telephone and internet traffic as almost a matter of routine. In 2013 the PRISM initiative of the US National Security Agency (NSA) and the Tempora programme of the UK's Government Communications Headquarters (GCHQ) were outlined in Snowden's files and showed how these agencies had almost unfettered access to user data from services such as Google and Yahoo, and the daily phone records of millions of telecoms customers. According to Snowden, 'I, sitting at my desk could wiretap anyone, from you or your accountant, to a federal judge or even the president, if I had a personal email' (Greenwald, 2013).

More concerning to many internet security experts was the revelation that the NSA and GCHQ had compromised the most widely used encryption systems, which had previously been thought to be secure even to prying from security services. Although arguments about preventing terrorist attacks can be made in support of these activities, there is a growing concern that the methods used to crack these encryption systems have undermined the ability of legitimate organizations and individuals to communicate in confidence. Questions of civil liberties and a right to privacy are obvious issues for debate. Former senior executive at the NSA and whistleblower Thomas Drake has been particularly critical of these activities and said the only way to avoid being watched by these agencies was 'to cower in a corner. I don't want to live like that. I've already lived that and it's not pleasant' (Buchanan, 2013).

Governments and security agencies have been intercepting private messages since the dawn of postal and telecommunications services over 100 years ago. What has changed in recent years to make this more of a concern for civil liberties campaigners is the extent to which we now realize this is taking place. There is a perfect storm of heightened concerns about terrorist threats, a massive upsurge in the volume of personal communications taking place over the internet, and advances in computing which allow the mass and automized monitoring of these messages. In the same way that we saw how companies like DataSift are tracking social media messages for organizations concerned about protecting their online reputations, so too are more secretive bodies such as the NSA and GCHQ to 'protect' national security and corporate interests. Whatever the rights and wrongs of Snowden's revelations at least we are now aware of the extent to which this is taking place and can debate the issues from a better informed position than before the leaks.

Helping the information flow both ways

Most research on open government has concentrated on how public bodies can either through choice or by statute make access to information easier; as we have seen, the internet has played a part in this. More recently interest has also been shown in how citizens and organizations outside government can use technology to feed information into public bodies. The growth of Web 2.0 and social media services has encouraged this development as more internet users expect to be able to interact online rather than simply be recipients in a one-way flow of information. In the UK in 2012 the COI produced a guide (COI, 2012) for civil servants on how best to engage with citizens using social media, which makes the claim that proper use of social media such as blogs, Facebook and Twitter could improve public engagement with government activities and save money in the process. Gibson believes that local government can make good use of social media to improve service delivery: 'Not engaging now represents a far greater risk than engaging. Citizens will still use these networks to talk about you, whether you add your voice to the conversation or not. . . . The challenge for all councils now is to move social media off their list of challenges, and on to their list of opportunities' (Gibson, 2010).

Gibson's observation that social media users will talk about public bodies online whether or not those organizations choose to take part is now becoming a fact of life in both the public and private sectors. When a local or national issue captures the public imagination there is now a variety of online places for the matter to be discussed, often to the detriment of those directly involved.

Engaging with others across social media is a challenge for many public servants and employees in the private sector. Posting information to websites and letting users take it or leave it is one thing, but soliciting feedback and taking part in online conversations is quite another. The COI guide is a response to this issue but it goes deeper than simply asking individuals to comment on aspects of government activity. The natural extension of these initiatives is to develop a far more responsive public sector that reconfigures many of its back-office functions and processes to adapt to an interactive digital world. This would be a move beyond services such as allowing users to renew parking permits online to giving citizens more direct involvement in policy making and driving the agenda of government. Initiatives such as e-petitions, set up by the British government, indicate where this may be going. The idea behind e-petitions is simple: any British citizen or resident can create a petition using the e-petition website and if it achieves more than 100,000 online signatures from other British citizens within a year the subject in question may be debated in Parliament. Launched in July 2011, more than 55,000 petitions had been lodged three years later although almost half of these had been rejected on the grounds that they had failed to meet e-petitions's terms and conditions.

While on the surface the e-petition initiative may seem like a good match of technology with democratic ideals, there are critics of the service who see it more as window dressing rather than a channel through which citizens can influence government policy effectively. Howard (2014) argues that it is the word 'could' in the phrase, 'If you collect 100,000 signatures, your e-petition could be debated in the House of Commons' which negates much of the initiative's value in representing a democratic ideal. She points out that even if petitions manage to pass the 100,000 signature hurdle they are only passed to the backbenches of Parliament and without support from an MP are unlikely to go any further. Even if it was guaranteed that all petitions with more than 100,000 signatures would be debated in the UK Parliament it is apparent that this would probably not overburden MPs. Of the almost 24,000 e-petitions that had closed by August 2014 after their one-year limit had been passed, only 28 had more than 100,000 signatures, and almost 10,000 of the petitions only attracted several votes of support from the public. Perhaps e-petitions are best viewed as an early experiment by government to try and harness the power of the internet to get closer to the electorate than as a finished product.

Making money from public information

The information industry has long relied on the public sector as a key primary source for many of the products and services that are sold to end-users. Company financial data, for example, originates in most countries from legal obligations placed on private enterprises to submit their annual and sometimes quarterly accounts to public bodies such as Companies House in the UK and, for publicly quoted companies, the Securities and Exchange Commission (SEC) in the USA. Weather data, property and land registrations, census information, data on industrial outputs and a raft of other information are a result of publicly funded operations. Putting a value on these activities is difficult as much of the information is given away or never leaves the organizations that collected it in the first place. Cross (2007) cites estimates which claim that the value of Ordnance Survey mapping data was worth £79 billion to the British economy in 2006 because of the range of industries that relied on it. Some have claimed this figure to be too high but even halving it leaves a very large sum and extrapolating it across other government departments indicates the importance of public sector information to the national economies.

A key debate among those concerned with public sector information centres is the extent to which public bodies should seek to maximize their financial returns by selling their information assets. On the surface it seems logical that the cash-strapped public sector should do all it can to achieve value for money for tax payers and if money can be raised from information buyers in the private sector then that course should be pursued. However, there are also strong arguments made that the public interest is better served in the longer term by public sector information being given away to interested parties who should then be free to turn it into commercial products and services. The rationale behind this argument is that more economic activity relating to job creation and tax receipts will be generated from a vibrant private market in developing information products than from short-term financial gains to public bodies through selling information. Evidence from European research carried out by consultants PIRA (2000) for the European Union would support the case for freeing up information exchange based on comparisons between European and US federal bodies. In the USA there has long been a tradition that information produced via the activities of the federal government should be freely available for third parties to use for commercial purposes. As a consequence a thriving market has developed that repackages financial, weather and mapping data to create paid-for information products.

Figure 4.1 presents a simplified comparison of the US and European public sector information models and shows the flows of money between the key

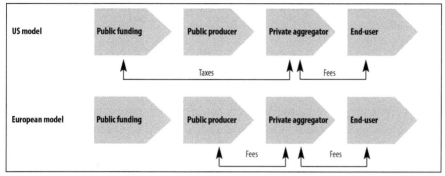

Figure 4.1 Models of public sector information re-use

stakeholders. The PIRA (2000) research estimated that in Europe, where government agencies typically charged for the data they produced, there was an average net financial return to the national economy of seven times the initial investment made by the agency in producing the data. However, in the USA, where no charges were made for the data, there was a net return of 39 times the initial investment. While this may seem a compelling reason for opening up the markets for public sector information there are also counter arguments that suggest agencies which are allowed to make a financial return on their information outputs are more likely to reinvest those profits into producing higher quality data sets. Agencies that rely solely on public funding for their operations, it is argued, will not have the resources to maintain such standards. In Europe the pressure for change resulted in a European directive in 2003 on the re-use of public sector information and this had been enacted into national laws by all EU members by 2008. Critics of the directive point out that, although its intention was to create a more vibrant public sector information market along the lines of the US model, its wording has allowed member states to avoid fully opening up their markets. A revised EU directive was passed in 2013 which strengthens some of the provisions of the 2003 legislation and goes some way to addressing critics of the previous one. The UK has been one of the more progressive EU members in applying the directive and in 2005 incorporated it into national law. Responsibility for ensuring that public bodies comply with the law rests with the National Archives, which has taken a proactive role in helping organizations adapt their information management practices to this new environment of greater data sharing.

   Advocates of greater data sharing by public bodies in the UK were given a boost in 2010 when the incoming Coalition Government created a Transparency Board whose responsibilities included 'establishing public data principles across the public sector and making datasets available for potential development and re-use' (National Archives, 2011). This was followed up in late 2011 when £10 million of public funding was put into supporting the Open Data Institute, a body set up to support UK companies that wish to re-use public information. Data will come from a range of bodies including weather data from the Met Office and house price data from the Land Registry. Although in the shorter term some of these bodies may suffer a loss of income from the commercial sale of data, in the longer term there may be broader benefits for the British economy and society. According to Hall (2011), 'the potential for the injection of up to £16 billion into the flagging UK economy could be too powerful a stimulus to ignore'. It is significant that the Open Data Institute is based in Shoreditch in East London, an area well known for its concentration of innovative, internet companies. Perhaps this signifies a belated but welcome recognition by government that information rather than just technology is at the heart of many of the innovative web services that are stimulating economic growth.

In 2013 the results of an independent study by consultants Deloitte into the UK's public sector information market were published. Deloitte estimates the direct value of public sector information at around £1.8 billion per year with wider social and economic benefits to the UK economy raising that up to around £6.8 billion (Shakespeare, 2013). The Shakespeare review, as the Deloitte study is known, does not go as far as some public sector information commentators would have liked. It does not recommend mandatory free access for everyone to all public sector data, but does acknowledge that faster and more consistent access to public sector information by private-sector companies would speed innovation in the UK's information sector. A significant initiative towards this objective has been the creation of the data.gov.uk initiative, which allows online access to public sector datasets for download and re-use for private or commercial purposes. The data is released under the Open Government Licence, which allows Crown Copyright information to be used in these flexible ways. This data portal and the Open Government Licence is probably one of the most significant changes to public sector information for a generation and, if the Shakespeare review report is correct, could stimulate economic activity worth billions of pounds. Four years after its launch data.gov.uk contained more than 19,000 datasets from a range of government and other public sector bodies. Perhaps more important than the total number of datasets are the types of data they contain. These range from expenditure data of local councils and road safety data to mapping and crime data. Mobile application developers have been some of the biggest users of this data using it to create apps to help with flood alerts, neighbourhood information and bus timetables. Globally, commercial enterprises see enormous value in unlocking the data kept hidden in public organizations. The consultant McKinsey estimates that if more countries followed the examples set by the USA and the UK more than US$3 trillion of economic value could be released annually (Chui, Farrekk and Jackson, 2014). It is impossible to test this estimate accurately but it indicates there is potential for the information sector to grow from the more open distribution of public data.

For the information profession these developments present an opportunity to take a more central role in public sector information management. While more traditional library-based roles may be cut back across many national and local bodies, the demand for information professionals with the skills to manage and manipulate data to comply with the new agenda for greater sharing is growing. These skills include an understanding of open standards for data management and how to allow sharing through application programming interfaces, breaking down the information silos that many public bodies have built up and which make sharing difficult. Developing these skills will require employers to change the training they offer their information professionals and librarians, and a reconfiguration of many of the library and information science courses that prepare graduates for information work.

Threats to the open web

At the beginning of this chapter the writer Jonathan Zittrain was mentioned in the context of his notion of the 'generative' nature of the internet. In his book *The Future of the Internet*, Zittrain (2008) explains why the internet has been such an important source of innovation over the last 20 years and why changes to the way the internet is managed and used may stifle future innovations. He points out that the network can be thought of as a series of layers, with the physical layer of wires, cables and routers at the bottom, overlaid by the protocol layer that allows the different components to talk to each other, and then an application layer whereby users interact with the internet via e-mail, web browsing, instant messaging and so on. Zittrain sees the separation of layers as crucial as it allows engineers, developers and innovators to work on the area they are specialists in without having to be experts in layers above or below them. The creator of the next successful social networking or internet search service does not need to have a detailed understanding of internet transport protocols or ask permission of the organizations that manage domain name servers or IP address allocations. These functions are independent of each other to the extent that control is distributed preventing any single organization from dictating who can gain access or what the network can be used for. His term for the defining feature of the internet, which has sparked such innovation across the communications and publishing industries, is 'generative': 'Generativity is a system's capacity to produce unanticipated change through unfiltered contributions from broad and varied audiences' (Zittrain, 2008, 70).

The internet has a high capacity for generating new services because it is a relatively open and freely accessible platform, which allows the creativity of others to flourish. We have seen earlier in this chapter how its predecessors such as CompuServe and AOL operated closed networks where users were only able to access services approved by the network owners. Such systems were not conducive to generating innovative services as there was a corporate filter that prevented most third party developers from entering. It is the 'unanticipated' part of Zittrain's definition above that is perhaps most significant: accurately predicting future technological developments is impossible, as to predict a new invention is effectively the same as inventing it. If anyone had anticipated the wheel before the first one had been made then they could be seen as its inventor. Similarly, in 1993 who could have foreseen how the web would have developed and what services it would spawn? Zittrain cites Wikipedia as an example of an unlikely service that has become a global resource used by hundreds of millions of people every week. Who would have anticipated that an online encyclopedia which relies on unpaid and unvetted amateurs to produce its entries would become a primary reference source? Would anyone have imagined that a 19-year-old student would develop a social networking service while still at university, which within ten years was regularly used by 1.3 billion people? Had CompuServe or indeed any other proprietary network had a say in those developments then it is unlikely they would ever have emerged.

However, Zittrain (2008) points to threats on the horizon to the generative capacity of the internet to stimulate future innovations. Some of these centre on the characteristics of modern internet devices and appliances, which are less open to hosting applications than a personal computer, and this will be looked at in the next chapter, which deals with information consumption. More relevant to our discussion here on information distribution are threats to the open nature of the internet as a platform for the free movement of digital bits. Whereas the ISPs, which transport internet traffic from web servers to end-users, have generally been agnostic as to what the data packets contain and given equal preference to Google's packets as any of its competitors, this may be changing. Network neutrality is the term that defines this notion of equal carriage and it has been a topic of heated debate among academics, legislators and network operators for several years. There is a fear that without adequate competition among providers of internet connectivity there may be a temptation for some companies to favour certain online services at the expense of others. Where an ISP is also a provider of telecommunication voice services, such as BT in the UK and AT&T in the USA, it is possible to see why they might not look very favourably on competing services such as Skype and Google Voice. Under those circumstances it might be tempting for some ISPs to degrade or block internet telephony services. In 2005 in the USA a small telecommunications operator, Madison River Communication, was found guilty by the regulator of preventing its internet customers from accessing internet telephony provider Vonage and fined US$15,000. Although this might be seen as evidence that, in the USA at least, regulators are enforcing the maintenance of a neutral and generative internet, there are growing arguments that new rules for internet governance need to be developed to prevent the subtle chipping away by commercial interests at the network.

The stakes are high for publishers and information providers as they come to depend increasingly on an open internet to distribute their content. Imagine the implications of a major media and news provider such as News Corporation entering into a commercial arrangement with a dominant ISP in the UK such as Virgin Media or BT. It would be technically possible for the ISP to give preference to News Corporation traffic and slow down traffic from its competitors such as the BBC or the Guardian Media Group. Over time this might discourage visitors to those sites as they find them less accessible than those from News Corporation. This is a hypothetical situation but not an unrealistic one. In 2010 the then UK Communications Minister Ed Vaizey was reported by Halliday (2010) as arguing in a conference speech that ISPs should be able to abandon network neutrality and allowed to provide preferential service to content providers that pay for it. While arguing on the one hand for an open internet, the minister also stated: 'We have got to continue to encourage the market to innovate and experiment with different business models and ways of providing consumers with what they want. This could include the evolution of a two sided market where consumers and content providers could choose to pay for differing levels of quality of service' (Halliday, 2010).

Vaizey's comments above appear to hold more sway in the USA than in Europe. In early 2014, after extensive lobbying by the telecommunications industry the US regulator appeared to concede that a two-tier internet might be desirable. As a consequence, Netflix revealed it was paying one of the country's largest ISPs, Comcast, additional fees to ensure its video content was delivered to customers at higher speeds than other content providers using the network. Several years earlier, mobile operators in the USA were exempted from net neutrality principles that had applied to fixed-line operators such as Comcast. In Europe, the mood among regulators is very different with the principles of open access and equal treatment for content providers becoming enshrined in legislation passing through national and European bodies. If regulators around the world settle on very different laws, as seems likely, then the ways that we as users 'experience' the internet will vary enormously depending on where we live.

The implications of a move to a more tiered level of service provision and pricing should be concerning for information professionals. The relatively even playing field that the internet has provided for information providers of all sizes has been a significant and positive development for information professionals. Never before has so much information been so freely available to so many and any developments which might take us back to a less open and more restrictive environment should be examined closely.

Concluding comments

This chapter has shown how new technologies and the legal and economic environments in which they operate are transforming the ways information is being distributed and the impact it is having on information creators, mediators and users. The internet is reconfiguring the information value chain and creating new opportunities for content creators to communicate directly with end consumers. Mobile networks are allowing users to break free of the constraints of buildings whether the home, office or the library, and the deployment of fourth generation mobile networks over the coming years will only accelerate this process as wireless download speeds could reach 1 Gbit per second. It is forecast that global mobile data traffic will increase elevenfold between 2013 and 2018 to 16 million terabytes a month (Cisco, 2014). The next chapter considers where all this data will end up and looks at the ways that users are consuming information, the devices and systems they are using, and what uses the information is being put to.

5
New models of information consumption

Introduction

Having looked at new ways that information is produced, distributed and
stored, this chapter will consider new ways that we are consuming
information. Ultimately, the way we consume information has not changed
over the years as it still relies on the sensory functions of our eyes and ears to
pass sights and sounds to our brains for decoding, processing and making
sense of. However, the methods and devices by which information now
reaches us have changed dramatically. An evolving ecosystem of hardware
and software is constantly struggling for our attention as we work, play, relax
and travel. Where time and location were once constraints on the types of
information we could access, these barriers are being broken down as devices
become portable and networks become pervasive. Giddens (1990) explained
the significance of this dislocation with his concept of time and space
distanciation whereby remote connections and interactions come to dominate
modern life. The first telegraph and telephone systems built in the 19th
century began this revolution, and more recent developments in computing
and mobile devices and networks have accelerated it.

   This chapter explores a range of issues surrounding these developments
and considers their implications for information professionals and the work
they do. The plethora of new information consumption devices is examined
within the context of the networks and information ecosystems that support
them. A central theme is the tension between organizations that are
attempting to exert control over these systems and those organizations and
users planning to develop a more open environment. This tension extends
the battles we have seen over personal computer operating systems and now
extends to mobile devices and the applications that run on them. We will look

at the discussions surrounding information overload and how, as some would argue, we are becoming unable to process all the information that is pushed at us from fellow workers, friends and social media contacts. Related to these discussions is the issue of information literacy and a concern that, while most of us can use the internet to find information, many people struggle to make sense of what they find. The opportunities for information professionals in helping users to develop their information literacy skills will be considered, as the role for many IPs is changing from information gatekeeper to facilitator. Finally, this chapter will look at how organizations are trying to make sense of the information that flows through their networks and consider whether the promises of knowledge management advocates from the late 20th century are finally being realized.

Information consumption devices

Perhaps the most visible evidence of the digital information revolution of the last 20 years is the devices through which we access these digital streams. This really got under way in the 1980s with the mass deployment of personal computers on workers' desktops and then into households. Deloitte (2013) estimates that the installed global base of personal computers was 1.6 billion in 2013. Before the rise of the internet most personal computers were either standalone devices or operated within a closed organizational network. Most of the information they processed was generated within the organization or household by the user or others on the network and consisted primarily of text documents or spreadsheets. Information professionals were among the first to access information remotely through the use of online databases and aggregators such as Dialog, Orbit and Questel. However, the complexities of creating a network connection and structuring search commands and the expense of subscriptions restricted their use to libraries and research institutes. A middle ground emerged in the 1990s when CD-ROMs emerged as a suitable media for end-user searching. A number of database providers offered their information on CDs that did not require networked computers; although often expensive to purchase, they removed the danger of inexperienced searchers running up large connection and download charges. Although a number of information vendors still offer CDs of their collections, that media and traditional dial-up access to online databases have been eclipsed by the internet as a distribution network and the world wide web as an interface to integrate online resources.

As we will see later in this chapter, these developments have had significant implications for many information professionals as access to online information has been opened up to the masses. Equally interesting is the lesson it provides for the benefits of open systems at the expense of more closed environments as a way to stimulate the diffusion of innovations. In the early days of online databases in the 1970s and 1980s, dedicated software and, very often, hardware were required to access the databases. On top of these requirements, the process for dialling in to the databases was often complicated and involved going through data gateways on the public telecommunications network. Once connected, the user had to use specific search terms and syntax that varied between databases with the result that most information professionals tended to focus on interrogating databases they were familiar with. The proprietary nature of these online systems restricted their diffusion throughout organiz-ations and it was not until a more open platform emerged in the form of the personal computer and the internet that online information became available to more end-users. The personal computer represented a multi-tasking device while the internet offered an open network to a range of data services beyond those offered by monopolistic telecommunications operators.

The evolution of the personal computer itself is a demonstration of how a relatively open system can win over a more closed one. The history of the personal computer and the battles between Microsoft and Apple over how a personal computer should operate are well documented, but it is worth reminding ourselves why for most of the last 30 years the personal computer, based on a Microsoft operating system, has been the dominant paradigm in personal computing. Although for most of 2014 Apple was the most valuable company by market capitalization on the planet, it should be remembered that in the 1990s the company was nearly forced out of the computing business. By the early 1990s the company had squandered its early lead in the personal computing sector by sticking to a closed model whereby the company sought to control the hardware and the software that ran on it. As a consequence, the range of Apple computers on the market was very limited, as was the software they could run, while personal computers running Microsoft's MS-DOS and then Windows dominated the desktop.

Key to the success of Microsoft was the fact that no single company had a monopoly on making personal computers, which were made from standard, interchangeable components. This encouraged hundreds of companies to start making personal computers, driving down prices and stimulating innovation as they sought to produce better machines. The only monopoly was centred on the operating system with Microsoft taking a licence fee for every legal copy of MS-DOS and Windows in use. Even though many would argue that Apple offered a superior product, the significantly lower price and wider choice of personal computers made them far more attractive to purchasers. Once an organization started using personal computers and the associated software, they became less likely to switch to another system such as the Apple Mac, creating a virtuous circle for Microsoft. The more people who used its software, the harder it became for a competitor to make inroads into the market. Organizations that have invested in training their employees on one operating system are reluctant to incur the costs of training them in another. These dynamics also work in the consumer market for technology where users become familiar with operating environments and are often resistant to change. Although Microsoft still dominates the market for desktop computing software, the rise of mobile computing devices seems likely to produce a more fragmented environment as hardware and software producers vie for our attention.

Mobile consumption devices

The personal computer coupled with the internet introduced the masses to online information consumption but it is the more recent developments in mobile technologies that are changing the expectations that many of us have about where and when information should be made available. Modern smart phones and tablet devices contain more processing power than a personal computer of only a few years ago and, by their nature, can be used in a far wider range of locations and situations. Figure 5.1 shows the relative global penetration of these devices by the end of 2014. More interestingly, it also shows the speed with which they have been adopted.

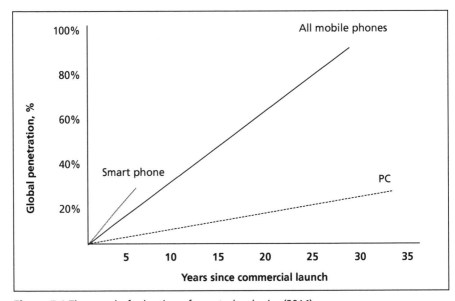

Figure 5.1 The speed of adoption of new technologies (2014)

Perhaps the first thing to notice from Figure 5.1 is the speed at which the mobile phone has been adopted in comparison with the personal computer. While it has taken over 30 years since the launch of the first mass-market IBM personal computer to achieve a global penetration of 22%, the mobile phone has been adopted by 96 out of every 100 people in the world in slightly less time. Smart phones, although a subset of the broader mobile phone market, are being taken up at an even faster rate. Seven years after the launch of the first Apple iPhone in 2007, smart phones were being used by approximately 25% of the global population, and according to Gartner (2014) accounted for 58% of all mobile sales in 2013. In this environment with most new mobile phones being 'smart', the term 'smart phone' has become almost meaningless. Increasingly, the same will be true of the term 'personal computer' as devices such as computers, tablets and phones become less distinct and start to replace each other for some purposes. Companies such as Hewlett Packard (HP) and Dell, which have traditionally focused on producing personal computers, are struggling to make the transition to this new world of mobile computing. However, it is the implications of the mass take-up of new portable devices for information consumption that is of most interest here.

According to the UK's Office for National Statistics (ONS, 2014), in 2014 there were 36 million mobile phone internet users across the UK. This figure doubled over the previous three years and illustrates a dramatic change in how many people are accessing the internet. According to the same report, 76% of all UK households in 2014 were accessing the internet every day, primarily from fixed-line connections over telephone and cable television networks. Almost all of these fixed connections were high-speed broadband ones with the older dial-up access method being shut down by the operator BT in 2013. Across most of the developed world these numbers are broadly similar with northern European countries tending to have the highest broad band penetration rates (OECD, 2014). What does this mean for how information enters the household? The key points are that most of us now have high-speed, always-on and, thanks to wi-fi and mobile broadband, mobile access to the internet. Therefore, two key parts of the infrastructure required for a true information society are in place at work and in the home: the networks to carry the information and the devices to present it to us. Although these networks will offer ever-faster connection speeds and the devices will become cheaper and more powerful, it is the final layer of the services that run over them which will be of most interest, particularly to information professionals. In Chapter 2 we saw how new content creators were emerging to take advantage of the digital information revolution and it is in the application layer that sits on top of these consumption devices that interesting developments are taking place.

Looking beyond the artefact

The digital revolution has spawned a plethora of devices that allow us to create, share and consume information in a variety of formats. Perhaps it was the launch of the iPod in 2001 that showed us what was possible when digitized and compressed content, in this case music, was combined with portable micro-electronics. Apple's advertising at the time promised 'a thousand songs in your pocket', which was a radical departure from the commonly used portable cassette or CD players, which could only hold a single music album at a time. While we now take it for granted that our music collections can go with us wherever we are, the iPod and similar devices broke down the restrictions of physical media such as tapes and CDs where there was a strong correlation between size and content. A tape-based Sony Walkman could never be any smaller than the audio cassette whereas digital music devices have become smaller while also increasing the amount of content they can store. By mid-2014 Apple's largest capacity iPod offered 160 gigabytes of storage, enough for 40,000 music tracks. Increasingly, even these devices are becoming redundant as smart phones become the preferred choice for listening to music on the move. Sales of iPods fell by 52% in 2013 from only a year earlier (Lee, 2014).

Although much media attention is focused on the shiny new devices that Apple, Samsung, HTC and others are flooding our shops with, it is important to look beyond the hardware at the software and content distribution systems that power them. Apple was not the first manufacturer of portable, digital music players but it was the first company to offer a device that linked to an easy to use and free piece of software, iTunes, which made transferring music from CD collections to the device a simple process. In 2003 the company also made it easier for consumers to buy and legally download digital music via the iTunes software, which extended the utility of Apple devices at the expense of the competition. Producing the best portable music player was no longer enough; it needed to be linked to software that allowed users' music collections to be managed via the personal computer and some form of online music store. Apple got this right at the beginning and effectively locked out its competitors through the use of proprietary software, exclusive deals with the music industry and its variation of the advanced audio coding (AAC) music compression format FairPlay. The company's success with this approach was quickly realized with iPods accounting for almost 90% of the US market by 2004 (Betteridge, 2004) and the term 'iPod' becoming a generic term for all such devices, similar to 'Hoover' for vacuum cleaners.

The amount of information iPods and similar devices provide is limited and primarily audio and video in content, the newer generation of smart phones and tablet computers can present a broader range of content. In some ways they are becoming the Swiss army knives of the digital age by encroaching on the territory of digital still and video cameras, music and video players, and some of the functions of the personal computer. The technical wizardry that allows devices weighing little more than 100 grams to shoot high definition video, store thousands of music tracks, surf the internet and make phone calls is impressive and an important factor for users' purchasing decisions. However, longer-term commercial success for device manufacturers will be driven by factors they may have less control over. These include the operating systems that power their devices and which, to a large extent, control the user interface. By mid-2014 there were two main smart phone software platforms: Apple's iOS and Google's Android. Together, these two platforms globally accounted for nearly 97% of all smart phones with Microsoft Windows, BlackBerry and 'other' platforms making up the rest (see Table 5.1) (IDC, 2014). Microsoft's 2.5% of the global smart phone market illustrates how dominating one computing market, the personal computer, does not guarantee success in another. Android's near 85% share of the market has more than doubled since 2011, and Apple's near 12% share has dropped from 18% over the same period. Apart from the growth of Android since 2011, the other notable trend demonstrated in Table 5.1 is the rapid decline of BlackBerry and 'other' operating systems, primarily Nokia's Symbian.

Table 5.1 The global smart phone market (mid-2014)					
Operating system	Market share	Market share change (2011–14)	Third party apps	Handsets	Handset manufacturers
Android	84.7%	+134%	1.3 million	18,000+	100+
iOS	11.7%	-37%	1.2 million	3	1
Windows phone	2.5%	+100%	300,000	17	4
BlackBerry	0.5%	-96%	235,000	10	1
Other	0.7%	-98%	n/a	n/a	n/a

Source: IDC, OpenSignal, company websites

As well as relative market shares, Table 5.1 also shows for each platform the number of apps available, and the numbers of handset manufacturers and individual models. Perhaps the most interesting differences are the number of different Android handsets available compared with the other four platforms. In mid-2014 there were estimated to be more than 18,000 different handsets from over 100 manufacturers. Accurate numbers are hard to determine because of the rapid growth in manufacturers, particularly in

China, which is a result of the open nature of the Android operating system. Anyone with the technical expertise can produce and sell an Android phone without having to ask permission of Google, whereas Apple tightly controls the production of iPhones and does not allow other companies to use the iOS operating system. The open nature of the Android platform can be seen as a vital factor in its dominance of the global smart phone market with handsets being produced for all types of customers from high-end £500 Samsung phones to sub-£50 phones for the budget end of the market. However, the success in growing market share has come at the expense of a unified experience for users. The freedom of manufacturers to produce thousands of different handset configurations and customize the software interface means that the experience of using a phone from one producer can vary greatly from that of using another's. This can cause confusion among customers who are often not aware what operating system they are using. Apple controls the hardware and operating system of its smart phones, creating a unified and consistent user experience. Both Google's and Apple's approaches have their advantages for users and manufacturers, and the data in Table 5.1 clearly illustrates the impact on sales.

For information professionals this presents a fascinating opportunity to observe how an important component of the emerging information society is developing. Will Apple make the same mistake it did in the 1980s with its Mac computer when it tried to control both the hardware and the operating system? Will Microsoft ever be able to replicate the success it had with its personal computer operating system software? Will the more open Android system allow Google to extend its dominance of internet search across mobile devices or will its fragmented nature be its undoing?

It's all about the apps

To be successful in the smart phone market a high-quality, feature-rich handset and an intuitive and responsive operating system are essential, but although those two characteristics are necessary they are no longer sufficient to ensure success. A third feature is a well populated application (app) store where third party software developers can upload the applications they have written for that platform and users can browse for free or low-cost downloads. Apple pioneered this concept in 2008 with the launch of its iTunes app store, which by the end of 2014 hosted over 1.2 million applications. Google's Android Marketplace was slightly ahead with more than 1.3 million apps. It is here that Apple has conceded that a relatively open system for encouraging the development of software is a benefit both to itself and its users. While the company sets rules for developers on how the apps must integrate with the iPhone, and vets new titles before releasing them through the iTunes store, Apple has created a software ecosystem and by the middle of 2014 more than 75 billion apps had been downloaded (Perez, 2014). The app store encourages the wider use of the iOS platform and iPhones, and is a major source of revenue for the company, with Apple taking a 30% commission for paid apps producing up to US$3 billion in revenue for the company in 2013.

The app stores and the titles they contain are a major factor driving the success of any smart phone operating system. For new entrants to this market or struggling platform providers such as Microsoft and BlackBerry, building and maintaining a vibrant app store is a key challenge. Third party app developers naturally produce software for the platforms with the most users, creating a virtuous circle for Google and Apple but a vicious circle for Microsoft and BlackBerry. This is commonly referred to as a network effect and it applies to many information and communication systems. In telecommunication systems the network effect can be seen as the network increasing in value to users as more people sign up as customers. In the early days of telephone networks there was little incentive for people to have phones installed in their homes because there were so few other people with phones for them to talk to. As the network slowly grew its customer base and people realized that friends and family were installing phones so the value of the network grew to hesitant subscribers. With smart phone platforms the network effect works from both the supply and the customer end with app developers ignoring less popular systems and users staying away from the platforms with smaller app stores. Apple was caught in a similar downward spiral in the 1990s when software developers were unwilling to produce applications for its computers that only had a market share of several per cent of computer users.

CASE STUDY Amazon

The online retailer Amazon has steadily built itself up from its launch as an online bookseller in 1995 to be the internet's largest department store, with a market value of more than US$157 billion by mid-2014 and annual sales of almost US$75 billion in 2013. Since 2005 the company has expanded its product range from books to include electrical goods, clothes, downloadable music and videos as well as creating a marketplace for other retailers to sell items. In this respect it can be viewed as a department store that sells items itself but also rents out space to in-store concessions. For information professionals its most important innovations have been in its integration of digital content and hardware devices for content consumption. Following Apple's success in reinventing music consumption with the iPod, Amazon has made a similar move for e-books. Its Kindle e-book reader has been an enormous success for the company and sold an estimated 10 million of the devices in 2013. In 2012 Amazon announced it was selling more e-books in the USA than paper copies in both the US and UK markets. While e-books and e-book readers have existed in various forms since the 1980s, the Kindle has finally brought them into the mainstream. The success is a combination of the e-ink technology in the devices that mimic the light-reflective qualities of paper and the Amazon online store, which makes purchasing and downloading books wirelessly a simple task. The launch of the colour screen tablet device the Kindle Fire in late 2011 signified a move by Amazon into other forms of content distribution via dedicated devices, particularly video and rich media. This was extended in 2014 with the launch of the Amazon Fire Phone that uses scanning technology to make purchases from the Amazon store easier for users. It seems that Amazon and Apple are on similar paths to create more vertically integrated technology and content distribution companies, developments that have significant implications for information consumers of all types. How far consumers will go along with this strategy is debatable as the trade-off for convenience and ease of purchasing and consuming information-based products is a more closed environment which restricts choice. Early evidence of poor Fire Phone sales suggests there is a lack of willingness to accept this compromise.

Information ecosystems: gilded cages or innovation hotbeds?

We have seen how two of the most successful technology companies, Apple and Amazon (see case study above), have created profitable businesses by making digital content easier for end-users to access and consume. Through their integration of e-commerce, software and well designed hardware they have managed to dominate the online music and e-book markets respectively. Apple's app store has encouraged thousands of independent software developers to create applications which, in some cases, have made their creators rich, although this is becoming more difficult as larger players move into this market. The Amazon Kindle provides a platform for anyone, with or without a contract from a publisher, to have their written works offered for sale. While the most successful Kindle titles are generally by mainstream writers who were already successful in the world of paper books, some new authors have managed to achieve hundreds of thousands of downloads without having a high profile in the traditional publishing world. E. L. James self-published her novel *50 Shades of Grey* on the Kindle platform in 2011 and within several years the three-book series had gone on to sell more than 100 million copies and was picked up by a mainstream publisher.

Similarly, John Locke has managed to sell more than 2 million copies of his books through the Kindle channel without going through a traditional publisher. He puts his success down to writing good page turners combined with an aggressive pricing strategy. Rather than the average US$10 that publishers were charging for similar e-books he decided to charge only 99 cents, on the assumption that his margins would be lower but higher sales would more than make up for that. Drawing on his commercial experience, Locke was attracted to the commission structure that Amazon offered: 'I've been in commission sales all my life, and when I learned Kindle and the other e-book platforms offered a royalty of 35 per cent on books priced at 99 cents, I couldn't believe it. To most people, 35 cents doesn't sound like much. To me, it seemed like a license to print money' (Barnett and Alleyne, 2011).

Although competing on price has worked for Locke it is not clear how sustainable such an approach would be for authors of less popular titles. It is undeniable that the Kindle platform has allowed Locke and other authors such as E. L. James to exert more control over how their works are published. Established publishers can be bypassed, stripping costs out of the book publishing value chain and allowing authors to keep more of the cover price and readers to pay less for the titles they buy. For proponents of the free flow of information and the democratization of ideas this seems like a positive move as barriers to information production and consumption are broken down, but there may be a price to pay for this digital nirvana and by the time this happens, it may be too late to do anything about it.

The e-books that Amazon sells for its Kindle devices are in a proprietary format, AZW, which contains a digital rights management element restricting what can be done with the e-book. These restrictions include the number of devices that users can read their downloaded titles on and the ability to lend copies to other Kindle owners. Apple imposed similar restrictions until 2009 on music downloaded from their iTunes store, which capped the number of iPods any individual user could play their music on. Content owners, whether music or book publishers, have often insisted on the use of digital rights management to protect their copyrighted material before agreeing to distribution deals with companies like Apple and Amazon. This is understandable when they can see the illegal downloading of their artists' works on a mass scale via P2P networks. The software industry has used similar measures such as unique product keys to try and control use of their products by non-paying users for many years. So while there is a business logic to restricting what users can do with content they have downloaded, the restriction presents a number of challenges to several established practices in the publishing world: fair dealing, resale and lending.

Fair dealing

Although its interpretation within the law varies between countries there is a general principle across most developed economies that copyright law needs to be flexible enough to allow certain exceptions. These exceptions typically relate to uses of copyrighted material for research, journalism, review and criticism. In its strictest sense, most intellectual property laws give control over what can be done with copyrighted materials to the copyright owner. For example, a literal interpretation of the law could prevent a writer, musician or film maker from allowing negative reviews of his or her book, opera or film from being published where extracts of the work were used to illustrate the review. Similarly, academic writers would need to obtain permission from any other author they were citing within their own writing. Strictly enforced, copyright laws would prevent library users from photocopying extracts of books or journals without permission of the copyright owner. Clearly, the enforcement of such rules would restrict intellectual discourse, academic research and basic journalism. It is for these reasons that the principles of fair dealing or fair use have emerged, whereby exceptions to copyright law are allowed to permit the exchange of ideas and the furthering of knowledge through development of the intellectual commons. In the UK this has typically been interpreted as allowing the copying of a single chapter of a book or an article from a journal for the purpose of research. However, the implementation of some digital rights management solutions to digital information has circumvented the fair dealing tradition by preventing even the modest copying of extracts of published works. In the case of the Kindle there are limitations imposed by the nature of the device itself; making a photocopy of a page on a Kindle is obviously rather difficult, but because it is a standalone device copying text from the hardware onto a computer is also restricted. Digital rights management within the e-books held on the Kindle also places restrictions on how much text can be exported and this amount can be set at zero, depending on the wishes of the publisher.

Copyright reformer and academic Lawrence Lessig revealed how digital rights management solutions can be implemented in a way that sweeps aside the notion of fair use with a few clicks of the mouse. In 2001 he was looking at an Adobe Acrobat e-book version of an out-of-copyright edition of *Alice's Adventures in Wonderland*, when he noticed that Adobe had set the permissions for copying sections of the text to, 'No text selections can be copied from this book to the clipboard' (Lessig, 2004, 152). Even if this edition had still been in copyright the principle of fair use would have applied but for a copy that was outside the copyright term such a restriction made no sense. While Lessig's example might seem trivial it demonstrates the power that digital rights management restrictions can place on content that would not be possible in the analogue world.

Resale

Although copyright owners across most economies are free to set the price at which the outputs of their creative endeavours are sold in the marketplace, this right is removed if the original purchaser decides to resell the book or music album. That, at least, has been the accepted practice across Europe and even enshrined in US copyright legislation. We probably do not even think about this aspect of intellectual property law and take it for granted that once we have purchased a legal copy of a book it is up to us what we do with it. It is hard to imagine having to seek the permission of the book's author or publisher before being able to sell it to our local book dealer or on eBay.

Applying these practices to the digital world is a little more complicated as the music files on our iPod or books on our Kindle create new problems for copyright owners. Although some publishers might resent not receiving a percentage of the income from second-hand book sales they can at least take comfort from the fact that a paper book can only be read by one person at a time. Digital copies of books and music, on the other hand, can be transferred between readers and listeners while still allowing the original purchaser to retain his or her copy. This obviously underpins the core rationale for digital rights management but it also stifles the resale market. With the Kindle, for example, the terms and conditions plainly state, 'Unless otherwise specified, Digital Content is licensed, not sold, to you by the Content Provider' (Amazon, 2014). This represents a fundamental shift in the relationship between publishers and readers and removes the right to sell on copies of works bought in the Kindle market. While it may be publishers and not Amazon who have driven this change in the sale of digital content, it is a landmark development that will have repercussions throughout the information sector and something we will come back to later in this chapter when we explore the notion of content renting rather than ownership. Even if the implications for information consumption are not as significant as this, it certainly spells trouble for second-hand bookshops if e-books continue to increase in sales.

Lending

At the heart of libraries of all kinds is the principle of lending materials, traditionally books, to users. From their foundations in the 19th century, public libraries around the world have sought to make reading matter available to those who could not afford to purchase books, journals or newspapers. Although the arrangements vary across countries, public lending rights have ensured authors receive compensation for the copies lent by libraries. Just as with the first sale principle described previously, purchasers of books have been free to lend them to whoever they wish without requiring the permission of the copyright owner. Although many libraries, public, academic and commercial, are incorporating e-books into their collections and grappling with the technical and legal issues of how they can be lent out, the situation is more complex for end-users. Amazon, as the world's largest retailer of e-books, is worth looking at again in this context with its terms and conditions stating: 'Unless specifically indicated otherwise, you may not sell, rent, lease, distribute, broadcast, sublicense, or otherwise assign any rights to the Digital Content or any portion of it to any third party' (Amazon, 2014).

In the USA it is possible, if the publisher permits, to loan a Kindle e-book to someone else for 14 days during which time the loaner is not able to read it. This does not seem to apply in other countries and the 14 day limit is rather restrictive.

So far this chapter has explored some of the business models that technology and content producers have been experimenting with when developing new models of information consumption. We have seen how Apple, Google and Amazon are attempting to integrate the hardware and software powering the digital devices that provide access to these new information superstores. At the same time these companies are also trying to encourage thriving ecosystems of developers to add value to the information consumption experience through app stores. We have also considered the potential downside to these innovations as content owners place new restrictions on what we can do with the information we have downloaded and the implications this might have for end-users and information professionals. The following section looks at some of the competing forces and technologies that may result in a less digitally locked-down future, which may be closer to the original aim of the world wide web's creator, Tim Berners-Lee, and his vision of it being a force for positive social change.

Returning to an open web

While the symbols of the digital revolution may be the smart phones, tablets and laptops that we carry with us, underpinning the radical changes to how we create, distribute and consume information over the last 25 years have been the internet and the world wide web. The internet has provided a relatively open platform across which digital information of all types can flow and the world wide web has given us an intuitive interface to interact with the information. Without those two developments, the shiny gadgets we crave and proudly show our friends would be useless objects, not able to access the music, films, e-books and other online content that gives them meaning. In Chapter 4 we saw how the open standards that define the internet and the world wide web have created a hotbed for innovation of all sorts, which would not have been possible had a commercial entity been in control of access for content creators and consumers. In some ways, the success of Apple and Amazon in the music and book publishing arenas represent attempts to pull back power from the anarchy of the open web and to control what can flow over the network and how such information is used. For some this has been a positive development as the user experience is tightly defined and allows less technically minded consumers, probably most of us, to pay for a generally fault-free consumption experience. However, there is a danger that by forfeiting some of the messiness of a more open web in exchange for easier access to the content we want we may be undermining the future of the web itself.

We have seen how the plethora of apps for mobile devices has been a key driver of smart phone adoption since 2008. The utility value of such phones and tablets increases with each new app as they extend the uses to which they can be put. Social networking apps allow users to easily keep in touch with friends; mapping apps integrated with GPS help us find our way; and content apps make consuming news and entertainment information a smoother experience than clicking across multiple web pages. While a discrete app may be a logical method for achieving a task such as navigation or document creation, in the same way that we use specific software applications on our personal computers to perform similar tasks, it presents problems when apps are used for information consumption. On a personal computer the web browser has become the dominant tool for accessing online information because it is content-neutral software that will present any information so long as it conforms to the open standards of the world wide web. We do not need to use separate browsers or applications to read information created by different publishers. The *Guardian* newspaper online can be read just as easily within any web browser as the *New York Times* online. However, the increasing use of apps by publishers presents a challenge to this situation, which could ultimately reduce the information choices of device users. Publishers, particularly in the magazine and newspaper sectors, are seeing sales of their printed editions steadily reducing as consumers spend more time looking for information on the internet. Maintaining content-rich websites has become the norm for such companies as they try to find ways to develop online revenue streams. Carrying advertisements and, in some cases, subscriptions on these websites are the most common ways of generating income but keeping visitors on their sites is always a problem when a competitor's content is only a click away. The walled garden of a dedicated app is one way of holding on to online readers as the publisher's content can be presented in a closed environment. Some commentators such as Zittrain (2008) see the increasing use of these apps for content distribution as a regressive step in the evolution of the information society. They argue that treating information islands that do not communicate with each other via web links will take us back to the pre-world-wide-web age of CompuServe and AOL. This should be a concern for information professionals as it has been the free linking between web pages that has advanced the creation, distribution and consumption of information more than any other invention since the invention of the printing press.

HTML5 – an antidote to appification?

Is the Balkanization of the world wide web through the widespread development and adoption of apps an inevitability or can something be done about it? Many argue that the fifth generation of the HTML web markup language HTML5 promises salvation from a fragmented web. Due to be fully recommended by the standards body, the World Wide Web Consortium, in late 2014, it is the first new version of HTML since HTML4 in 1997. HTML5 offers a number of improved features and innovations for web developers, with significant improvements in how it manages multimedia such as video and audio and the ability to work with cached, offline data among the most important. Developers are currently taking advantage of these features to create HTML5 apps that can work across personal computer and smart phone platforms. Such apps have the appearance of a discrete application but are run within the traditional web browser. These are the advantages for developers:

- The app only needs to be written once and will work across any device capable of running a modern web browser.
- Content presented within HTML5 is indexable by search engines and so can be found by users.
- As with traditional HTML, content can be mashed with other sources to create information-rich pages.
- The bottleneck of the app store can be circumvented as HTML5 content can be distributed across the open web.

For publishers the cross-platform compatibility of HTML5 brings cost-savings in application development, which allows more resources to be put into creating better content. Opening up content to search engines can result in higher visitor numbers, which could be seen as a counter to the attraction, to some publishers, of traditional apps as walled gardens where they have more control over how their information is consumed. Whether HTML lives up to the expectations of its proponents is still in mid-2014 uncertain but the economic benefits it promises to publishers and the visibility it offers to search engines make it at least in theory an attractive development platform. The *Financial Times*, a global financial newspaper, certainly believes in the promise of HTML5 as a way to push its content over mobile devices. In 2011 it made a strategic decision to bypass separate app development for different mobile platforms and used HTML to deliver its news and articles. According to Dredge (2013), within two years one-third of the newspaper's web traffic was coming in via mobile devices. For the *Financial Times*, a major benefit was the cost-saving of not having to develop and maintain apps for different platforms, but the main advantage was not having to pay a sizeable proportion of so-called 'in-app' purchases to either Apple or Google. In-app purchases are financial transactions that take place between the user and the app developer once the app has been installed. Such purchases are particularly prevalent in online games such as Candy Crush where users often pay to move up levels of play and buy extra features. Although these can be very profitable for the app developer they can also generate large revenues for the app store owner, which charges commissions of up to 30% of the transaction fee. For content creators such as the *Financial Times* these charges over the course of a customer life-cycle can have a significant impact on bottom-line profits. By allowing users to install the HTML5 app directly from the Financial Times website this issue is avoided.

Burley (2011) expands on the challenges that publishers face when repackaging their content for the tablet and smart phone era and the need to offer consumers more than just the same information in a fancy new package: 'For publishers this means knowing and anticipating audience needs, having a thorough understanding of all available content, including content from public databases, and having a nimble infrastructure that allows disparate types of content to be "mashed together"' (Burley, 2011).

Burley's suggestion that publishers should make better use of third party information to create value-added mashups is not a new one but is radical in that it requires a different mindset from the traditional publishing model, which focuses on control over published outputs. In Chapter 4 we saw how public sector bodies are becoming more proactive in making their data available for others to use. Burley recommends that publishers might do well to integrate this information into their offerings. The opportunities are significant, particularly where publishers combine the value of such information with the functionality of new mobile devices.

The experiential web

We can begin to see how this might work with the rise of augmented reality mobile devices such as Google Glass and Oculus Rift (see case study below). These wearable technologies are perhaps the next stage in the evolution of mobile computing. Although still as of mid-2014 in an embryonic stage, they allow users to see digital overlays of the physical world; in the case of Oculus Rift, there is a 3D environment that wearers can immerse themselves in. The opportunity for content publishers to provide relevant, contextual information to users wearing such devices is significant. Having to type search requests into a smart phone may seem antiquated within a few years when smart glasses may be able to anticipate and project the information you seek in front of your eyes before you even know you need it. That certainly is the goal of Google, although privacy concerns and public resistance to such an immersive information environment may restrict its ambitions.

CASE STUDY Oculus Rift

The Oculus Rift virtual reality headset has its origins in 2012 when its developers launched a prototype of the device aimed at games developers, using funds raised by the crowd-funding website Kickstarter. Originally intended to provide an immersive 3D experience for gamers the technology behind Oculus Rift has the potential for use in a broader range of information consumption settings. This potential was recognized by social media company Facebook, which paid US$2 billion for the company behind the headset in early 2014. Whereas Google's wearable glasses aim to deliver information to users via discrete eyewear, the Oculus Rift is designed to allow users to explore virtual 3D worlds. For gamers this is a natural evolution from the traditional video display and a technology, which a number of companies have unsuccessfully attempted to develop over the last 20 years. However, the applications for this device extend far more widely to areas such as online training, virtual tours of cities and buildings and exploring virtual worlds. While the virtual online world Second Life never lived up to expectations following its launch in 2004, other similar initiatives may be more successful when experienced via 3D goggles. Success for Oculus and other similar initiatives will be dependent on the imagination of the content creators who deliver their information via these devices and the willingness of users to wear them.

Rent or buy?

The question whether to rent or buy has faced those looking for a home for generations. It is also increasingly becoming a question for information consumers as the options for accessing content, particularly entertainment, increase. For the first 30 or so years of television we only had the option to watch programmes as they were broadcast with no accessible mechanism for recording video content to watch later. Since the 1980s we have been able to rent or buy video cassettes and then DVDs and record programmes on our own devices. Similarly, books have been available to buy in shops or borrow from libraries. Like television programmes, music was accessible over the airwaves or could be bought in the form of records, tapes or CDs. For those producing entertainment content, whether film, music, video or printed, the period since World War 2 has generally been profitable. As we have seen in previous chapters, the channels for distribution were limited and the ability of consumers to circumvent those channels restricted by the analogue technologies of the day. However, the digitization of the content and the networks that carry it have opened up new opportunities to break free of previous constraints. This has led to the illegal downloading of billions of music tracks, which, according to many in the music industry, has decimated the recording sector. The figures are stark: a 33% decline in recorded music sales in the UK between 2001 and 2011 and a 50% decline in the USA (Economist, 2011). Although iTunes and other legal music downloading services have provided welcome revenue streams for publishers, they have not made up for the declining revenues delivered by falling CD sales.

Perhaps the future for content industries lies not in trying to replicate the past with digital business models that mimic how we used to consume information. While downloading music from iTunes is a very different way of purchasing music, it still rests on the assumption that consumers wish to own their digital purchases. For some this is undoubtedly the case but an increasing number of consumers seem happy to move away from the ownership model to one that is more transient. Content streaming services have been gaining in popularity, particularly for music. These include services such as Pandora, Last.fm and Spotify (see case study below), whereby users have access to hundreds of thousands of music tracks that can be streamed over the internet to personal computers and mobile devices. Netflix (see case study in Chapter 4) and Amazon Instant Video offer similar services for video content.

CASE STUDY Spotify

The music streaming service Spotify was launched in 2008 by Swedish founders and by early 2014 had more than 40 million users, 10 million of whom paid monthly subscriptions. One of the key drivers of success for the company has been the range of music available with over 20 million tracks available to users. Users on free accounts have access to the whole catalogue but are restricted in how the service works on mobile devices and must listen to adverts. Premium account holders can download up to 3333 tracks to a mobile device without being interrupted by adverts. As smart phones become more prevalent and mobile broadband a standard service for most users, in developed countries streaming services such as Spotify are likely to become more popular with users. However, as we saw in Chapter 4 they are not always so popular with musicians as royalty payments are very low. Although Spotify offers an on-demand radio experience for its users, the service does not provide a similar benefit that traditional radio did for music copyright holders. While royalties are paid to such holders when their music is played by radio stations, there was the added benefit that listeners would often then purchase the music providing an additional revenue stream for musicians. With Spotify there is no need for users to purchase tracks they like as they can be streamed on demand.

In Chapter 4 we considered the economics of these services for publishers and artists, and the revenues from streaming looked very different from those generated by CD sales. From an information consumption perspective the rise of streaming services presents some interesting challenges to how we think about the ownership of content. We have already seen that purchasers of e-books on the Kindle platform do not own a copy of the book in the same way they do with paper copies, but instead are licensing the content. Music and video streaming extends this further, with the content, passing through the devices of most subscribers and only existing to the user for the length of the playback. A major benefit of streamed content for users is having access to far larger libraries than they could ever own if they had to pay for and download each track or video, and streamed content presents the opportunity for content owners to overcome digital piracy albeit generating smaller revenues on their assets than in the pre-internet era.

Making sense of it all

We know that the world has never before been presented with so much information and being able to keep on top of the demands it places on us, and to sort the wheat from the chaff, is a growing problem for information professionals and the end-users they serve. Before the arrival of personal computers on every desktop and then their connection to the internet, information professionals were often the gatekeepers to information resources. Now that role is changing to being more of a guide and teacher, helping users navigate and find the information themselves.

Information literacy

Anyone who works in education will have a view on the impact the internet has had on how young people learn. Some will bemoan the rise of the Wikipedia generation, which finds instant information gratification from a Google search, while others point to the richness of the resources to which students now have access at home and school. In recent years there has been a growing debate about the longer-term impacts that the internet is having on how all of us think about information and ideas. Some such as Carr (2010) believe that there is a downside to having so much information on tap and that it is diminishing our ability to think more deeply about ideas and concepts as we flit from one web page to another. In 2008 Carr provocatively titled an article in *The Atlantic*, 'Is Google making us stupid? What the internet is doing to our brains'. He questioned whether in our embrace of the web we are losing the important faculty of critical thinking. Carr's account of how he uses the internet as a resource is honest and chimes with many of us who can remember a pre-internet age:

> For more than a decade now, I've been spending a lot of time online, searching and surfing and sometimes adding to the great databases of the Internet. The Web has been a godsend to me as a writer. Research that once required days in the stacks or periodical rooms of libraries can now be done in minutes. A few Google searches, some quick clicks on hyperlinks, and I've got the telltale fact or pithy quote I was after.
>
> (Carr, 2008, 57)

Whether Carr's hypothesis that being able instantly to locate a nugget of information reduces the longer-term development of our intelligence is correct is a debatable point and not without its critics. Lehrer (2010) does not disagree with Carr that our lives are becoming a constant stream of interruptions from the computer screen as messages and notifications ping at us from a variety of sources, but argues this might not be such a bad thing. Citing research from the University of California, Lehrer claims that having to analyse and process large amounts of information quickly through the interrogation of internet search engines actually stimulates brain activity and could be seen as making us smarter. This is an ongoing debate; whatever the outcome, it seems unlikely that we will return to a previous age where research required days spent in libraries poring over books. The internet and whatever succeeds it offer faster access to more information than could ever be found in a single library collection of printed materials, and the challenge for information professionals and educators is to help students and users make the best use of them.

This challenge has led to the development of research into helping people, particularly students, with their information literacy skills. Anyone can type a search request into Google and click on the results, but being able to decipher those results and make a reasoned judgement on what is appearing on the screen requires critical skills not always apparent among students at schools and universities around the world. According to the American Library Association (ALA): 'To be information literate, a person must be able to recognize when information is needed and have the ability to locate, evaluate, and use effectively the needed information' (ALA, 1989).

The ALA definition of information literacy extends the parameters beyond simply decoding search results and incorporates the ability for users to know which situations require information and then what to do with it once the right information has been found. The ALA's UK equivalent, the Chartered Institute of Library and Information Professionals (CILIP), produced a similar definition of information literacy in 2004; the subject has become a priority area for the professional body: 'Information literacy is knowing when and why you need information, where to find it, and how to evaluate, use and communicate it in an ethical manner' (CILIP, 2004).

CILIP's definition builds on that proposed by the ALA by introducing the notion that information literate people should have an understanding of why the information sought is required and be able to communicate the findings in an ethical manner. In a practical sense one of the challenges that educators and librarians face is persuading students and users that there are other research resources besides Google and that any information found needs to be evaluated critically for its relevance and provenance. As anyone who has attempted to do this will testify, it is not always an easy task.

One of the leading bodies in the UK that has looked at the issues of information literacy and how to address it within the context of higher education is the Society of College, National and University Libraries (SCONUL). In 1999, SCONUL introduced the concept of the Seven Pillars of Information Literacy, which has since been taken up by educators and librarians around the world (SCONUL, 1999). Acknowledging how the digital landscape has changed how students look for, access and use information, SCONUL updated and extended its Seven Pillars model in 2011 although the basic principles of the original model still apply. One of the driving factors behind SCONUL's work in this area has been the recognition that information handling skills are different from skills in using information technology. This has often been an area of confusion for policy makers who have often equated an ability to use a personal computer and associated software with being information literate. SCONUL, drawing on research by Corrall (1998) and others, has disassembled these processes to show the context within which the tools such as computers fit in the broader information landscape. As all of us, not just students, increasingly access and consume information through digital devices, the understanding of how we make sense of this information through research by organizations such as SCONUL will become more important. Educators, information professionals and policy makers need to be able to see beyond the devices and help users evaluate the information that flows through them.

One of the challenges educators have in helping students develop their information literacy skills is the lack of awareness among information seekers that these skills are actually important. Research from UK media regulator Ofcom (2013) shows that among children aged 8 to 15 the most frequent use of the internet is to do school homework; perhaps surprisingly, it is used for this purpose more often than for social networking, downloading music or instant messaging. When the children involved in the research were asked how much they trusted the websites they used to help with their homework, just over 90% of them stated that they believed all or most of the information they found was true. Nearly one-third (30%) of the 12–15-year-olds believed that if a website was listed in search engine results then it must be true, and about one-sixth (17%) of this age group stated that they did not think about the reliability of search engine results and just used websites which they 'liked the look of'. This unquestioning trust in search engines and the websites found through them is concerning; many educators find it difficult to counteract it.

This task of improving the information skills of students may become more complex as the services we use online develop and begin to deliver results and information tailored to our previous behaviour. In a similar way that Amazon gives us recommendations based on items we have already purchased, so too Google presents search results based on what we have previously searched for, sites we have visited and the physical location from where we are searching. Therefore identical searches performed by different people on different machines may produce differing results. Google is making decisions about the information it thinks is relevant to us as individuals rather than simply responding to a search request. In theory, this is an attractive proposition as our information needs are often based on the context in which we are looking for that information. If Google can better understand that context then we are likely to be served more relevant results, but not everyone is enthusiastic about this and other similar developments across the plethora of internet-based information services. Pariser (2011) believes such developments can be limiting and refers to the phenomenon as the 'filter bubble'. One of his criticisms centres on the importance of being exposed to a variety of information sources and opinions rather than simply those we are comfortable with: 'Consuming information that conforms to our ideas of the world is easy and pleasurable; consuming information that challenges us to think in new ways or question our assumptions is frustrating and difficult' (Pariser, 2011, 88).

There is a danger that users of these information services will be unaware of the filtering that is taking place and assume that the information they are being presented with is representative of the broader universe of data that exists on the open web. So rather than simply showing users how to perform better searches, a role for many information professionals will be to help information seekers better understand what is going on in the backend systems of Google, Facebook, Amazon and other internet services.

Information overload

In the space of approximately 20 years most developed economies have moved from an era of relative information scarcity to one of abundance and, some would say, overload. Three hundred years ago most of the information that people processed was sensory information related to their surroundings and the people they interacted with. As reading skills improved and books and newspapers became more widely available, new forms of information were assimilated into the daily lives of individuals. Radio and television in the 20th century added to this so that by the 1990s most households consumed a variety of printed and broadcast content with many white collar workers also processing information via personal computers. As we have seen over this and previous chapters, the internet and its associated services and devices have added a new layer on top of those analogue sources, with mobile networks providing access almost wherever we are.

Measuring how much information exists is an almost impossible task as assumptions need to be made about what is being measured. For example, estimating the storage required to digitally store a book requires decisions to be made about whether the digital copy would be a scanned, facsimile copy or simply a reduction of the contents into an Ascii file that would be considerably smaller. However, attempts have been made, and despite issues around accuracy they show that the information available to us in a variety of formats has grown faster than most commentators imagined. In 1997, Lesk (1997) estimated that there existed several thousand petabytes (1000 terabytes) of information globally and in 2000 Lyman and Varian (2000) calculated the world was producing between one and two exabytes (1000 petabytes) of unique information annually. By 2018, internet switch manufacturer Cisco (2014) estimates that the amount of information flowing across the internet globally will be 1.6 zettabytes, much of which will be the data that flows across our computer and mobile phone screens. To put that into perspective, 1.6 zettabytes is the equivalent of approximately 3000 trillion books or the contents of 156 million US Libraries of Congress.

Clearly, a lot of this information sits on computer servers and is never presented to humans for processing by our limited intellects and attention spans, but a significant proportion goes into the e-mails, web pages, RSS feeds, Facebook updates and tweets that are constantly pinging at us from our phones and computers at home and work. Market research company Radicati estimates that an average of 183 billion e-mails were sent every day in 2013, approximately 26 e-mails daily for every person on the planet (Radicati Group, 2013). Coping with this tsunami of data is becoming a burden for many of us and a variety of tools and methodologies have emerged to try and wrest back control. Chui et al. (2012) found that office workers spend an average of two and a quarter hours a day dealing with e-mail and argue that this is having a negative effect on productivity at work. Hemp (2009) believes the e-mail problem at work is perpetuated by workers sending out too many unnecessary messages to colleagues. As well as helping workers process e-mails more efficiently, a solution Hemp suggests is to 'encourage them to be more selective and intelligent about creating and distributing information in the first place' (Hemp, 2009, 87).

Perhaps one of the most widely used systems for coping at a personal level with the digital age is the Getting Things Done (GTD) methodology developed in the USA by David Allen (2002). At the core of Allen's GTD system is the acknowledgement that the human brain is excellent at innovative and creative thinking but is poor at storing and recalling information. Allen argues that relying on our brains and not a trusted system to store information causes us stress through the worry that we will forget things that need to be done. His solution is to create a system, paper or computer-based, that will act as the storage system for our to do lists and project files, freeing our minds to engage in more creative thinking and finding solutions to issues at home and work. The plethora of software that claims to be GTD-compliant, the GTD training courses that take place around the world and the hundreds of thousands of copies of Allen's book that have been sold suggest there is significant demand for a solution to coping with information overload.

Implications for information professionals

Just as mobile phones allowed users to make calls away from their homes and desks, changing the way we think about communications, so too is mobile broadband impacting on the distribution of information. The ability to access and transmit information while on the go is changing how many information workers operate and creating new industries in the process. As information access is untethered from physical spaces, the impact on libraries, already affected by the rise of the fixed internet, may become more pronounced. Mobile communication technologies make the possibility of information being available anytime, anywhere, to anyone closer than ever, and institutions operating within the scarcity model of information provision and expecting users to visit their premises may become less relevant. On the surface this may appear to be bad news for the traditional library, particularly public ones. However, the wireless revolution may also present opportunities as mobile workers look for new places to work. Cassavoy (2011) quotes a freelance worker who prefers to work out of coffee houses in the Austin, Texas, area: 'I am the type of person who would go crazy without being around other people. Working from home or a rented office would get lonely fast.'

A frequent discussion among library professionals in recent years has been whether libraries should change their configuration to appeal to a broader range of users. Within academic libraries this has resulted in areas set aside for group working, social meetings and the serving of refreshments. Waxman et al. (2007) discuss their research into what students want from libraries and conclude that the creation of more convivial surroundings including the introduction of coffee bars can encourage more students into university libraries. Others are less convinced by such developments, particularly when it applies to public libraries. Clee (2005) acknowledges that libraries need to change to remain relevant in the 21st century but fears that some libraries 'appear to have settled for becoming community information points with coffee shops attached'. Whether appealing to coffee addicts is the right strategic move for libraries is debatable, but offering a working environment such as that favoured by Cassavoy's mobile worker above may be sensible for some. Certainly, libraries as physical spaces are changing particularly in academic institutions. In 2014 Florida Polytechnic University (FPU) opened its new library which did not contain a single physical book. Students using the library have access to over 135,000 e-books. Echoing concerns about information literacy expressed earlier in this chapter, the head of library services at FPU stated, 'The ability to read, absorb, manage and search digital documents and conduct digital research are skills of growing importance in industry', with the new digital-only library 'designed to help students become better technology users and learners' (Flood, 2014).

Concluding comments

In this chapter we have seen how the rise of computing devices, deskbound and portable, and the information ecosystems that surround them are changing the ways we consume information. These changes present opportunities for publishers, information professionals and end-users to improve the way we work and are entertained. However, they also lead to challenges as we attempt to cope with the interruptions that these devices bring and the sheer quantity of content that needs to be processed and made sense of. While we are still coming to terms with this brave new digital world it is inevitable that solutions to educating users in information literacy and systems for dealing with information overload will be found and adopted. Perhaps more interesting are the implications for information production. In Chapter 2 we saw how new technologies are leading to new models of information production, and in some ways we have come full circle. As social media and interactive publishing platforms such as blogs encourage readers to add their thoughts and comments, so a new layer of richness is added to the original content. The story does not necessarily end as the journalist's work goes to the printing presses but lives on as readers post their views to the web either directly to the newspaper's website or indirectly via platforms such as Facebook or Twitter. For information professionals this increases the sources they need to keep track of as the boundaries of the reference world move beyond the journal and the online database.

6
Conclusion

Introduction

We have seen in the preceding chapters how the digitization of information is transforming a number of industries including book, newspaper and music publishing, and changing the roles and responsibilities of those who manage information within organizations. Although there is a danger for industry commentators and analysts to overplay the role of technology in influencing organizational and societal change, an objective of this book has been to show that real changes are under way. Examples and case studies have been used to illustrate how established organizations are responding to these challenges and how new companies are being formed to take advantage of them. Alongside the focus on organizational change has been a consideration of the impact these developments are having more broadly on the work of information professionals. This concluding chapter will bring together some of the themes and issues already discussed and examine what they might mean for information workers, publishers and, more broadly, society in the second decade of the 21st century.

The struggle for control in a networked world

In both the public and commercial sectors there is a tendency for organizations to grow in the scale and scope of their operations. Pioneering companies such as Ford and General Motors realized that economies of scale achieved by increasing production would allow them to produce their cars at a lower cost, making them more competitive in the marketplace. Governments have tended to follow this pattern as well as most politicians and civil servants, despite what they claim in public, preferring to extend the reach of their operations. This is not necessarily to criticize this tendency; lower prices for consumers should generally be seen as a good thing and larger government departments may be able to deliver public services more efficiently. In 1937 the economist Ronald Coase (1937) pointed out that the primary reason individuals act collectively under the umbrella of the firm is to reduce transaction costs. These are lower when managed within an organization than when carried out by and between individuals. Coase's theory explains the rise of large enterprises since the industrial revolution, particularly during the 20th century. However, with the rise of the internet at the end of the last century economists began to wonder whether a digital world might be governed by different rules from those described by Coase. Notions of a 'weightless economy' where the free flow of information across devices connected by the internet might change generally accepted economic principles were developed (Quah, 1996). Why, some more enthusiastic commentators argued, would we need the monolithic corporations that had thrived in the 20th-century world of atoms when we were moving into a world of bits where transaction costs would be zero? Some 25 years after the birth of the world wide web, these claims now feel rather hollow. It could reasonably be argued that the upstarts born out of the internet are now the giants of the information economy. As we have seen in previous chapters, Google, Amazon, Facebook, their older siblings Apple and Microsoft, and a host of rapidly growing companies are leading innovation and social change. Perhaps Coase's theory holds as true today as it did 80 years ago, except maybe corporations are growing in size faster than ever.

There seems to be a tendency for these internet giants to grow in the scope of what they do as well as in size. As we have seen, Amazon has evolved from being an online seller of books to running the world's largest department store with a rapidly growing media and technology arm. Google no longer just provides an efficient search engine but also acts as the leading global platform for digital advertising, the driving force behind the most widely used smart phone operating system, Android, and the repository for tens of millions of scanned books. Facebook may be the world's most popular social network but it is also expanding into virtual reality and the delivery of broadband to parts of the developing world. If we do live in a world where, according to Mandel (2012), 'data-driven economic activities' are driving economic growth then these companies are at the vanguard of this revolution.

Implications for information professionals

It seems strange that at a time when the wealth of developed economies is increasingly dependent on information industries, the jobs of many information professionals are under mounting pressure, and in some sectors under threat. Cuts to public libraries around the world since the credit crunch of 2008 have been widely reported and academic and school libraries have also been under financial pressure to do more with less. Why are many of the professionals trained to manage information not reaping the benefits of the information revolution? A major reason is the move from analogue information artefacts such as books, newspapers and journals to digitized formats that have required new technical skills not traditionally taught on the academic courses accredited by professional bodies such as CILIP and the ALA. Another factor has been the mass adoption of internet access in households and the accessibility of cheap computing devices. These developments have allowed many people to find the information they need at home rather than calling on the services of libraries and information professionals. However, as we have seen in the preceding chapters the rise of new models of information production, distribution and consumption has also offered opportunities for information professionals to capitalize on their skills.

The knowledge management opportunity

Some readers will remember the knowledge management boom of the 1990s when every technology vendor from IBM to Microsoft was claiming how their systems would allow companies to capture the collective knowledge of their employees. Tapping in to these knowledge bases, it was claimed, would give a company a competitive advantage over its competitors, as knowledge replaced capital as the way to dominate a market. Researchers and analysts such as Davenport and Prusak (1998) and Nonaka and Takeuchi (1995) presented compelling cases for the ability of organizations to capture, store and make accessible their employee's knowledge for use in the creation of new products and services, and to improve the efficiency of business processes. For many information professionals at the time it seemed an opportunity to move into roles more closely aligned with their employers' core business and the not insignificant chance to increase their salaries. The initial promise of many knowledge management tools and techniques was never realized though, and the phrase took on rather negative connotations often associated with the dot.com bust of the early 2000s. Tom Wilson's (2002) article 'The Nonsense of Knowledge Management' exposed many of the unsupportable claims made by knowledge management advocates and extended the debate on whether knowledge is actually manageable.

Although the term fell out of favour with many information professionals for a number of years at the beginning of this century, there has been something of a resurgence more recently. Just as the rise of Web 2.0 tools and technologies such as blogs, wikis, social media and RSS have helped rejuvenate the technology sector, so too have they raised hopes that this time the technology might be able to deliver on earlier promises. An easy to deploy and cheap tool such as a wiki allows organizations to share information between employees easily; while it is debatable if this could be called knowledge sharing, it certainly provides a platform for a collective repository of useful information. Levy (2009) and Lee and Lan (2007) have shown how the collaborative nature of many Web 2.0 tools lends itself to the principles of knowledge sharing and that many of the modern tools are more user-friendly than the systems of the 1990s. Davidson (2011) argues that the power of these tools to help organizations better share knowledge aligns well with the core competences of many information professionals and presents opportunities for them to apply their skills in this new environment. One of the advantages of modern tools such as wikis and other collaborative platforms is that many of them are easy to experiment with outside the workplace, allowing users to become comfortable with them before making the case to managers for a more formal roll-out. Solutions that are hosted outside the organization and in the provider's 'cloud' may require less assistance from IT support staff, making deployment less expensive and demanding on internal resources.

A common feature of these new collaborative platforms from vendors such as Jive, IBM, Huddle and Microsoft is their incorporation of social tools including messaging, file and image sharing and personal status updates, which bear similarities to public social network services such as Facebook and Twitter. This has led some commentators and vendors to badge these products as 'social business' tools. Whether they will live up to the promise of making corporate life a more social affair that encourages knowledge sharing remains to be seen. A cynic might see this as simply a repeat of the tendency for vendors to rebrand their software as knowledge management tools 20 years ago.

The future of search

We know that Google has changed the way most of us look for information to the extent that the verb 'to Google' someone or something is now commonly used. It was Google's use of counting links between web pages as a key factor in determining results that set it apart from other search engines and has given it a near monopoly in internet search. The implications of this for information professionals have already been discussed but it is worth considering how people's searching habits may change in the future.

One of the complaints often levelled against search engines such as Google is that they only present users with links to web pages that the provider thinks are relevant based on the search terms appearing on those pages. It is still up to the searcher to click on those links and find the information on the resulting pages. This can be frustrating for searchers who simply want an answer to a specific question. As a result, Google launched in 2012 what it calls its Knowledge Graph, which takes information from selected reference sites including Wikipedia and presents snippets of data from those sources in the search results. This may include text, images and numerical data and is an attempt to provide enough information so that the searcher does not have to click through to individual web pages. Google extended the Knowledge Graph service in 2014 with its Knowledge Vault, which according to Hodson: 'has pulled in 1.6 billion facts to date. Of these, 271 million are rated as "confident facts", to which Google's model ascribes a more than 90 per cent chance of being true. It does this by cross-referencing new facts with what it already knows' (Hodson, 2014).

Google's Knowledge Vault and similar initiatives from other web technology companies are attempts to provide semantic search capabilities for users whereby search engines better understand the intentions of searchers. These technologies are spilling over into the world of smart phones with voice-activated search services including Siri on iOS and Google Now on Android devices. While the technologies are still in their infancy, the ability of the services to learn by analysing which results are acted on by users could allow them to rapidly evolve. As smart phones become ubiquitous and embedded in the daily lives of users this 'machine learning' will accelerate to produce information retrieval services that will make the traditional Google search look antiquated. Google is not the only company attempting to provide specific answers to questions rather than millions of links to web pages. The Wolfram Alpha web service, which calls itself a computational knowledge engine, launched in 2009 and draws on structured data sets from a variety of sources to provide precise answers to questions. For example, the question 'will it rain tomorrow?' produces tables of local weather forecast data and the percentage chance that it will rain tomorrow. The company claims that its service draws on over 10 trillion pieces of data from primary sources and uses more than 50,000 types of algorithms and equations to manipulate the data when responding to queries. Although it is efficient at providing answers to questions which have unambiguous answers, it is far less useful in helping choose a new camera or book a holiday where judgement becomes a factor. However, for some of the questions that a typical public library reference desk receives, the service certainly can be a viable substitute.

Ninja librarians

We saw in Chapter 2 how social media services such as Facebook and Twitter are producing new forms of information, which are becoming a valuable data resource for researchers and marketers. Other groups interested in mining this data are the security services that monitor the social networks to gain insights into the activities of individuals and organizations in which they have an 'interest'. Hill (2011) describes how a CIA office in the USA employs several hundred analysts, who describe themselves as ninja librarians, to track the social media sphere. While security services around the world have been monitoring electronic communications for many years, it is only recently that they have been able to eavesdrop on the open communications that take place across social media services. Hill (2011) points out that the 'ninja librarians' were able to track and predict developments in the Arab uprisings of 2011 by looking in aggregate at the tweets and Facebook postings of those involved and observing events on the street. Although these analysts are not librarians in the traditional sense of the word, it is interesting that they have co-opted the term to describe their activities; this perhaps indicates an evolution of the description for people who work with information.

Not many organizations have the resources of the CIA to employ hundreds of people to monitor traffic on social networks but an increasing number would like to have that capability. One of the approaches to allow this has been the development of sentiment analysis, which uses computer algorithms to infer meaning from digital text. Although any search engine can create an index of web pages based on the words it finds, their proximity to other words and its interpretation of the main keywords, none of them can yet effectively and accurately determine what it means in a human sense of understanding. Artificial intelligence systems and natural language processing research has made significant inroads in this area but human language and its textual representation are still too nuanced for computers to fully understand what the author is saying. However, services exist which claim to be able to offer an interpretation of the sentiment of digital messages, especially social media content. These are of particular interest to companies wishing to monitor their reputations online across a range of websites, discussion forums and social media. By receiving an early warning that negative discussions and comments might be emerging online, a company can evaluate what can be done to address those issues, such as responding to adverse comments or putting right problems with its products or services. The British marketing analysis company Brandwatch offers a range of services for companies wishing to track what people are saying about them online: 'Our sentiment analysis is based on a library of hundreds of rules, which are used to define whether a mention of your search term(s) is positive or negative in tone' (Brandwatch, 2012).

Such a product is similar to press cutting services used by organizations for many years to track what is being said about them and their competitors, but allows humans to be removed from the equation. A traditional press cutting service, even when the collection stage is automated, requires people to read the news stories and interpret what they mean for the client and, crucially, whether it is positive or negative reporting. A service such as Brandwatch can present the client with a summary of what is being written across a range of online sources and interpret the meaning. Following an exhaustive and detailed analysis of a number of sentiment analysis technologies, Pang and Lee (2008) conclude that although there is still much work to be done in improving the accuracy of the underlying technologies, it is possible for organizations to obtain reasonably accurate and useful results. The logical conclusion of developments in natural language processing and sentiment analysis tools is the removal of the need for people like the CIA's ninja librarians whose judgement is currently relied on to interpret the disparate streams of information flowing across the internet. Just as the search engine has undermined the perceived value of the library reference desk, perhaps Siri, Wolfram Alpha and Brandwatch will remove the need for the information professionals and analysts who make sense of the information once it has been retrieved.

By this stage, if you are a librarian, library student or another kind of information professional, you might be thinking of throwing in the towel and considering another line of work or study. If that is the case, then think again, as while new technologies undoubtedly make some tasks and roles obsolete, they also create new ones. In the spirit of adding the 2.0 suffix to new ways of working, MIT academic Andrew McAfee coined the phrase Enterprise 2.0 to describe the changes taking place in the ways that organizations are restructuring to take advantage of new computing technologies (McAfee, 2009). As an explanation for the key processes underlying the evolution of Enterprise 2.0, McAfee created the acronym SLATES, which stands for Search, Links, Authorship, Tags, Extensions, Signalling. At its core, SLATES describes the processes by which information is produced, classified, distributed and then found by employees and uses a range of modern technologies such as blogs, wikis, RSS and other tools that facilitate information creation and exchange. What immediately should stand out to any information professional is that these are the very tools and processes that are at the heart of much information work: classifying information, sharing it and helping others to find the data they need. If McAfee is correct that successful enterprises of the future will need to focus on developing these areas and competences, then perhaps the outlook for information professionals is bright.

Implications for publishers

In previous chapters we have seen how new technologies of information production and distribution are transforming the publishing industry across a range of media types. Cheap computing devices and the internet have lowered the barriers to entry for anyone who wants to build a publishing empire. For some established companies this challenge is proving particularly difficult to overcome and newspaper publishers in particular are seeing reduced sales and profits. Although new content creation companies such as BuzzFeed and GigaOm described in Chapter 2 are making inroads into the media landscape it should be noted that traditional publishers are not all sitting on their hands. They recognize that change is inevitable and that their business models will have to adapt to the digital media landscape. Hyams (2011b) argues that in their attempts to make this change publishers are becoming technology providers by developing platforms more friendly to digital distribution and consumption through computing devices. She points out that this is particularly the case among academic publishers, who are formatting their content for use on e-book readers and developing new purchasing models, including the rental of e-textbooks. While renting a key text may be cheaper for students, according to Hyams it also cuts out the resale of second-hand books for which publishers receive no income.

As these new models and technologies evolve it is inevitable that some will fall by the way and others will become established practice. Whether they will continue to generate similar profits for publishers, as the traditional models of book and journal publishing have done in the past, remains to be seen. A large driver of success will be the extent to which they fit with the consumption habits of digital consumers who increasingly expect to find the information they need when they want it and in a format that is convenient. Pearson and McGraw-Hill, two of the world's largest academic publishers, are moving their business models to this new form of delivery. According to industry analyst Outsell, the US market for school and college textbooks was worth US$12.4 billion in 2012 with just over one-quarter of that being spent on online resources including e-textbooks (Simon and Will, 2013). As academic libraries increasingly move away from paper books to digital resources and the trend for streaming information rather than owning it continues, it seems likely that the renting of textbooks will probably soon overtake owning them.

The copyright challenge

One of the reasons that many publishers have been slow to adapt to the digital landscape is the fear of piracy. As we saw in Chapter 4, the music industry is still struggling to develop new business models that can cope with the rise of illegal music downloads via websites such as The Pirate Bay. Although there are rigorous debates over the extent to which piracy has been directly responsible for the travails of the music industry, it is undeniable that digitized content is far more easily copied and distributed than analogue formats. The deployment by publishers of digital rights management software that restricts the amount of sharing and copying of content consumers can do has been one response to this problem. The rise of streaming media services whereby consumers pay a fixed monthly fee for access to music, which ceases when the subscription ends, is another response. What links these attempts to enforce intellectual property rights in a digital world is a belief among the content owners that existing copyright laws must be maintained and that the new technologies must fit within that legal framework.

An alternative approach has been to question whether our ideas on the ownership of ideas and content need to adapt to the new models of information production, distribution and consumption. In Chapter 5 the example was given of how an e-book version of an out-of-copyright text, *Alice's Adventures in Wonderland*, had been locked down with digital rights management to the extent that, under the terms of the licence, the book could not be shared, given away or read aloud. The source of that example was a Professor of Law at Harvard University, Lawrence Lessig. His criticisms of copyright legislation in the USA and other developed economies led, with the help of others, to the creation of an initiative known as Creative Commons, a non-profit organization which offers licences to content creators outlining how their works can be re-used. Creative Commons licences are not designed to replace the ownership rights inferred by copyright legislation but to offer a more flexible approach for the re-use of original content, whether music, writing, videos or images. Content owners can choose from a variety of licences that range from only allowing their creations to be used for non-commercial uses to the free re-use for any purpose, including commercial re-use, provided that author attribution is made. It is not known exactly how many works have been released under the initiative but in mid-2014 the photo sharing website Flickr was hosting more than 300 million photos whose owners had assigned Creative Commons licences (Flickr, 2014). In the broader picture of the creative industries this is a relatively small number and the licences have been used largely by smaller, independent artists and authors, but the Creative Commons ideals are significant because they offer a new way of thinking about intellectual property.

Just as open source software projects are transforming important segments of the technology industry, albeit rather slowly, so the Creative Commons initiative and whatever follows it are creating a grassroots movement of change among content creators. In 2009 Wikipedia, one of the world's most visited websites, adopted a Creative Commons licence for all the content it hosts. In the networked and interconnected world of information we are now entering the old models of locked-down content that suited the analogue production and distribution models look less sustainable.

Hooked on tablets

We saw in Chapter 5 how new portable computing devices are changing the ways many of us use consume information, in particular news. By 2014, almost two-thirds of all UK adults had a smart phone and nearly half of all UK households had a tablet computer, with similar figures for the USA (Ofcom, 2014). These findings are significant because of their implications for the information sector and, for tablets in particular, because they show how rapidly a new information consumption device can be taken up; the first tablet computer, the Apple iPad, was only launched in 2010. For those concerned with so-called 'digital divides' between older and younger computer users, Ofcom research shows that tablets are driving a rapid growth in web usage among the over-65s. Many newspaper and magazine publishers see the tablet as a potential saviour in the light of falling circulations and advertising revenues from their print operations. Some publishers have developed apps for the presentation of their content, for example, *The Economist* app offers a reading experience of content on a tablet similar to that of reading the printed magazine.

Another approach has been the development of apps such as Pulse and Flipboard, which aggregate content from a variety of publishers and present it as a form of news stand where users can pick and choose which sources to read. Some of these services also integrate social media streams and RSS feeds to create a mashup of sources from traditional and online-only publishers. Part of the appeal of apps like Flipboard that offer this functionality is the clean interface they offer users rather than the more cluttered and confusing presentation of RSS readers, which have never had mass appeal. The failure of pure RSS readers to catch on with the mass market was demonstrated by Google's decision to close down its RSS Reader service in 2013. The challenge for publishers will be to find ways to generate revenue from presenting their content in tablet-friendly ways. While this has proved very difficult, and impossible for some, on the open web it is hoped that consumers will be willing to pay for content if presented in a user-friendly way. With tablets this challenge may be easier for publishers as the mechanisms for handling payments are already in place. Apple, a key producer of tablet devices, already handles payments from millions of consumers via its iTunes service.

Google, the company behind the Play Store for Android, also handles financial transactions for app sales, and a new entrant to the tablet market, Amazon, is the world's largest online retailer. Although the mechanisms for taking payments are in place, concerns among publishers may develop into a fear that some or all of the three companies just mentioned will become monopolistic gatekeepers to consumers in the same way that many music publishers feel Apple has done with iTunes and music sales. In the short term at least, publishers probably have little choice but to adapt to the world of tablets, phablets and smart phones and their associated app ecosystems.

Implications for society

Throughout this book we have seen how the new models of information production, distribution and consumption are changing the ways publishers manage their operations and information professionals deal with the new types and formats of information that their users require. However, it should be remembered that many of these changes are having broader impacts on society at large. When most people come to rely on the internet as the primary platform for finding and consuming information then any changes to the way that platform operates will have consequences for all of us. We saw this in Chapter 4 with the issue of net neutrality and the threats to the relative openness of the internet posed by competing commercial interests. As technology becomes more embedded into our work and social lives, the decisions of regulators, politicians and companies such as Google and Apple can shape the trajectories of innovation and development of the networks and devices we rely on.

Internet everywhere

The endpoints of the internet are generally the web servers that hold the content and the devices through which we access that content. For the consumption of information by individuals this has worked very well, but imagine a future where inanimate devices such as your fridge, car or even a can of baked beans can send information over the network. At a basic level this already occurs in many libraries with the automatic checking in and out of books via the radio-frequency identification (RFID) technology embedded in chips inside books. Tales of intelligent fridges that can automatically order food for you when they detect the milk or eggs are running out have been circulating since the internet became a fixture in households. However, the rise of low-cost computer chips, mobile internet connections and the deployment of virtually unlimited IP addresses via IPv6 are making this a more realistic possibility. According to Miller and Bilton (2011), Google is one of the companies that are investing millions of dollars in researching the development of such smart devices via its secret laboratory known as Google X. In Chapter 2 we saw how serious the company is in this regard with the spending of several billion dollars on a maker of domestic thermostats and fire alarms.

Although the examples described above are perhaps relatively trivial, the implications of such a development are significant, particularly for businesses that are keen to streamline their processes such as stock and inventory control. If a warehouse or factory can automatically order stock items as they run low, it could transform the manufacturing process and reduce inefficiencies and waste. Chui, Löffler and Roberts (2010) imagine a not too distant future where pills can be ingested and send back images of the body they are passing through to help with medical diagnoses, and billboards will scan pedestrians and show advertisements they consider appropriate for the audience. The extent to which the internet will become embedded in the everyday items all around us remains to be seen, but it is inevitable that where a business case can be made for it then companies will be keen to exploit the potential of the internet of things. One of the results of this will be a massive increase in the amount of data flowing through the internet as billions of items are sending out signals to remote listening posts.

Nowhere to hide

Another issue to be considered if the internet of things becomes a reality is the impact on personal privacy. While our local supermarket might like to know our fridge is running low on milk and needs to order some more, we might not be so comfortable giving up this information. When the internet is everywhere how much autonomy will we retain when our devices are taking control of our lives? This is already becoming an issue with location-aware smart phones and some of the services that take advantage of this capability. Smart phone apps increasingly seek to access the GPS data from users' phones to add to the other data they already collect and send back to the cloud. This is a marketer's dream, with information about our preference for cafés, shops and hotels being sent out to a range of companies, sometimes without our knowledge. Alongside the data we share across social networks and via search engines, some of the larger internet companies are building up detailed profiles of our friends, where we work, what we like and where we go.

As the largest social network, Facebook and its more than 1.3 billion users is a prime target for privacy campaigners. The company has probably not helped itself in this respect with its frequent and sometimes confusing changes to the default privacy settings it ascribes to users. A starting point for many organizations that need to screen job applicants is the social web, where online profiles can tell a potential employer whether or not to send out an invitation for interview. Services such as Klout (see case study in Chapter 2) and Kred, which apply numerical scores to the social media profiles of individuals based on their activity and who they are connected to, are taking this to the next level. Just as web pages rely on the Google PageRank algorithm for their visibility in search results, so too might we be judged in the future by our social media score, which will determine where we study and who will employ us. The Chartered Institute of Personnel and Development in the UK reports that almost half of employers look at an applicant's social media profile before deciding who to shortlist for interview (CIPD, 2013). When decisions are increasingly made by computers, and computers work best with unambiguous, numerical data, then perhaps our worth will be decided by an algorithm.

Concluding comments

The breadth of subjects and issues covered in a book of this length has inevitably resulted in a broad overview and discussion of some of the new models of information production, distribution and consumption. The intention has been to introduce readers to some of the key technologies that are changing the ways information is created and found, and the implications these changes have for information professionals, publishers and society. We are seeing a restructuring of the information industries with many publishers becoming technology companies and technology giants such as Google encroaching on the territory of a range of content producers. Just as the invention of the printing press over 500 years ago helped usher in the Age of Enlightenment, which radically changed how we looked at our world, so too may the new digital technologies of content production and distribution transform the world in the 21st century. Brooke (2011, ix) certainly shares this view and is optimistic that digital technologies can have a benevolent impact on society: 'Technology is breaking down traditional social barriers of status, class, power, wealth and geography, replacing them with an ethos of collaboration and transparency.'

Perhaps an age where information is everywhere and accessible to everyone will help us overcome some of the challenges the planet faces as global warming and economic and political uncertainties require new ideas and ways of thinking. Whether the emerging models of information production, distribution and consumption are moving societies towards such an age of openness remains to be seen. There are powerful interests, political and economic, that would like to use the digital revolution to extend their control over markets and citizens. In this respect, many of the emerging technologies present a double-edged sword: Google and Facebook may know more about us than we would like, but equally they provide a window to a wealth of information resources that can help us make better and more informed decisions. For new and useful information services to evolve on the platform that is the internet we all need to be cautious and remember how the world has become so connected in such a short space of time. The threats to a relatively free and open internet are real for the reasons we looked at in Chapter 4 and a return to locked-down communications networks controlled by the commercial interests of network operators should be resisted by all information professionals. Tim Berners-Lee, the inventor of the world wide web, sums up what we have to lose:

> The web is now a public resource on which people, businesses, communities and governments depend. It is vital to democracy and now more critical to free expression than any other medium. It stores and allows us to share our ideas, music, images and culture. It is an incredibly intimate reflection of our interests, priorities, disagreements and values. That makes the web worth protecting.
>
> (Berners-Lee, 2014, 87)

I could not agree more.

References

Abram, S. (2007) The Future of Reference in Special Libraries Is What Information Pros Can Make It, *Information Outlook*, October, **35**.

Accenture (2013) *Mobile Web Watch 2013: the new persuaders*, www.accenture.com/SiteCollectionDocuments/PDF/Technology/accenture-mobile-web-watch-2013-survey-new-persuaders.pdf.

AdNews (2012) *ABC Circulation Results*, November 2012, http://yaffacdn.s3.amazonaws.com/live/adnews/files/dmfile/ABC_circulation_Sept2012.pdf.

ALA (1989) *Presidential Committee on Information Literacy: final report*, American Library Association, www.ala.org/ala/mgrps/divs/acrl/publications/whitepapers/presidential.cfm.

Allen, D. (2002) *Getting Things Done: how to achieve stress-free productivity*, Piatkus Books.

Al-Nakaash, P. (2011) *The Future of Content Aggregation*, white paper, LexisNexis, www.lexisnexis.co.uk/media/insights/The-Future-of-content-Aggregation.pdf.

Amazon (2014) *Kindle License Agreement and Terms of Use*, www.amazon.com/gp/kindle/kcp/install.html?ie=UTF8&mobile=1&tou=1.

Andrade, P. L. et al. (2014) From Big Data to Big Social and Economic Opportunities: which policies will lead to leveraging data-driven innovation's potential? In *The Global Information Technology Report 2014*, World Economic Forum.

Andreessen, M. (2014) *The Future of the News Business: a monumental Twitter stream all in one place*, http://a16z.com/2014/02/25/future-of-news-business/.

Babcock, C. (2006) Data, Data, Everywhere, *Information Week*, 5 January, www.informationweek.com/shared/printableArticle.jhtml;jsessionid=E1BNEBPSPXE1JQE1GHPCKH4ATMY32JVN?articleID=175801775.

Baker, J. (2014) *The British Library Big Data Experiment*,
http://britishlibrary.typepad.co.uk/digital-scholarship/2014/06/the-british-library-big-data-experiment.html.

Barnett, E. and Alleyne, R. (2011) Self Publishing Writer Becomes Million Seller, *Telegraph*, 21 July, www.telegraph.co.uk/culture/books/booknews/8589963/Self-publishing-writer-becomes-million-seller.html.

Battelle, J. (2006) *The Search: how Google and its rivals rewrote the rules of business and transformed our culture*, Nicholas Brealey.

BBC (2014) *Facebook Emotion Experiment Sparks Criticism*, 30 June,
www.bbc.co.uk/news/technology-28051930.

Beaujon, A. (2014) *New York Times Digital Subscriptions Grew 19% in 2013*,
6 February, www.poynter.org/latest-news/mediawire/238583/new-york-times-digital-subscriptions-grew-19-in-2013/.

Bell, D. (1973) *The Coming of Post-Industrial Society: a venture in social forecasting*, Basic Books.

Bentley, J. (2011) A Good Search, *Information World Review*, September/October, 14–15.

Benton, J. (2014) *The Leaked New York Times Innovation Report is One of the Key Documents of this Media Age*, 15 May,
www.niemanlab.org/2014/05/the-leaked-new-york-times-innovation-report-is-one-of-the-key-documents-of-this-media-age/.

Berners-Lee, T. (2014) Tim Berners-Lee on the Web at 25: the past, present and future, *Wired*, March, 86–101.

Betteridge, I. (2004) iPod Market Share Falls to 87%, *PC Magazine*, 4 November, www.pcmag.com/article2/0,2817,1712062,00.asp#fbid=irDZQ7jrChJ.

Bintliff, E. (2011) Emap Boosted by Online 'Intelligence', *Financial Times*, 31 January, www.ft.com/cms/s/0/d8dcaf2a-2ca8-11e0-83bd-00144feab49a.html#axzz3HdkmErrD.

Brandwatch (2012) *Sentiment Analysis*,
www.brandwatch.com/wp-content/uploads/2012/11/Sentiment-Analysis.pdf.

British Library (2011) *The British Library and Google to Make 250,000 Books Available to All*, 20 June, www.bl.uk/press-releases/2011/june/the-british-library-and-google-to-make-250000-books-available-to-all.

Broady-Preston, J. and Felice, J. (2006) Customers, Relationships and Libraries: University of Malta – a case study, *Aslib Proceedings*, **58** (6), 525–36.

Brooke, H. (2011) *The Revolution Will Be Digitised: dispatches from the information war*, William Heinemann.

Buchanan, M. (2013) How the N.S.A. Cracked the Web, *New Yorker*, 6 September, www.newyorker.com/tech/elements/how-the-n-s-a-cracked-the-web.

Budnarowska, C. and Marciniak, R. (2009) How Do Fashion Retail Customers Search on the Internet?: exploring the use of data mining tools to enhance CRM,

15th Conference of the European Association for Education and Research in Commercial Distribution (EAERCD) held on 15–17 July 2009, University of Surrey, (unpublished).

Burley, D. (2011) *To 'Appify' Old Media, We Need a New Approach*, 17 January, https://gigaom.com/2011/01/17/to-appify-old-media-we-need-a-new-approach/.

Cane, A. (2009) The Final Frontier of Business Advantage, *Financial Times*, 27 November, 2–3.

Carlson, N. (2010) AOL Insider Says TechCrunch Price Only $25 Million – CNBC Says $40 Million, *Business Insider*, www.businessinsider.com/aol-techcrunch-price-25-million-2010-9.

Carr, N. (2008) Is Google Making Us Stupid? What the internet is doing to our brains, *The Atlantic*, **301** (6), 56–63.

Carr, N. (2010) *The Shallows*, Atlantic Books.

Carroll, E. and Romano, J. (2010) *Your Digital Afterlife: when Facebook, Flickr and Twitter are your estate, what's your legacy?*, New Riders.

Cassavoy, L. (2011) Starbucks Is My Office: a guide for mobile over-caffeinated workers, *PC World*, 18 April, www.pcworld.com/businesscenter/article/225471/starbucks_is_my_office_a_guide_for_mobile_overcaffeinated_workers.html.

CFoI (1998) *Lord Chancellor Presents 1997 Freedom of Information Awards*, Campaign for Freedom of Information, 28 April, https://www.cfoi.org.uk/1998/04/lord-chancellor-presents-1997-freedom-of-information-awards.

Chui, M., Löffler, M. and Roberts, R. (2010) The Internet of Things, *McKinsey Quarterly*, Issue 2, 70–9.

Chui, M. et al. (2012) *The Social Economy: unlocking value and productivity through social technologies*, McKinsey & Company, www.mckinsey.com/insights/high_tech_telecoms_internet/the_social_economy.

Chui, M., Farrekk, D. and Jackson, K. (2014) *How Government Can Promote Open Data and Help Unleash Over $3 Trillion in Economic Value*, McKinsey & Company, www.mckinsey.com/insights/public_sector/how_government_can_promote_open_data.

CILIP (2004) Information Literacy: definition, Chartered Institute of Library and Information Professionals, www.cilip.org.uk/cilip/advocacy-awards-and-projects/advocacy-and-campaigns/information-literacy.

CIPD (2013) *Recruiting and Pre-employment Vetting in the Social Media Era – CIPD publishes new guidance for employers*, press release, 9 December, www.cipd.co.uk/pressoffice/press-releases/recruiting-pre-employment-vetting-social-media-era-cipd-publishes-new-guidance-employers-91213.aspx.

Cisco (2014) *Cisco Visual Networking Index: forecast and methodology, 2013–2018*, www.cisco.com/c/en/us/solutions/collateral/service-provider/ip-ngn-ip-next-generation-network/white_paper_c11-481360.pdf.

Clarke, R. (2000) *Information Wants to be Free*, www.rogerclarke.com/II/IWtbF.html.

Claussen, J., Kretschmer, T. and Mayrhofer, P. (2013) The Effects of Rewarding User Engagement: the case of Facebook apps, *Information Systems Research*, **24** (1), 186–200.

Clee, N. (2005) The Book Business, *New Statesman*, 21 March, www.newstatesman.com/node/150243.

Coase, R. (1937) The Nature of the Firm, *Economica*, **4** (16), 386–405.

COI (2011) *Reporting on Progress: central government websites 2010/11*, Central Office of Information, www.gov.uk/government/uploads/system/uploads/attachment_data/file/62661/reporting-on-website-progress-Oct2011.pdf.

COI (2012) *Social Media Guidance*, Central Office of Information, www.gov.uk/government/publications/social-media-guidance-for-civil-servants.

Corrall, S. (1998) Key Skills for Students in Higher Education, *SCONUL Newsletter*, Winter, 25–9.

Cross, M. (2007) Public Sector Information 'Worth Billions', *Guardian*, 15 November, www.guardian.co.uk/technology/2007/nov/15/freeourdata.news.

Darnton, R. (2013) The National Digital Public Library Is Launched!, *New York Review of Books*, 25 April, www.nybooks.com/articles/archives/2013/apr/25/national-digital-public-library-launched/.

Davenport, T. and Prusak, L. (1998) *Working Knowledge: how organizations manage what they know*, Harvard Business School Press.

Davenport, T. H., Harris, J. G. and Morison, R. (2010) *Analytics at Work: smarter decisions, better results*, Harvard Business School Press.

Davey, J. (2009) Every Little Bit of Data Helps Tesco Rule Retail, *Sunday Times*, 4 October, 7.

Davidson, C. (2011) *Designing for Flow: part 2 – new opportunity, new role and new tools*, http://futureready365.sla.org/11/01/designing-for-flow-part-2.

Dellavalle, R. P. et al. (2003) Going, Going, Gone: lost internet references, *Science*, **302** (5646), 787–8.

Deloitte (2013) *The PC Is Not Dead*, www2.deloitte.com/za/en/pages/technology-media-and-telecommunications/articles/tmt-technology-predictions-2013.html.

Dishman, L. (2011) *Innovation Agents: Jeff Dachis, founder, Dachis Group*, Fast Company, www.fastcompany.com/1716575/innovation-agents-jeff-dachis-founder-dachisgroup.

Dormehl, L. (2014) Internet of Things: it's all coming together for a tech revolution, *Observer*, 8 June, www.theguardian.com/technology/2014/jun/08/internet-of-things-coming-together-tech-revolution.

Dredge, S. (2013) Financial Times: 'There is no drawback to working in HTML5', *Guardian*, 29 April, www.theguardian.com/media/appsblog/2013/apr/29/financial-times-html5-no-drawbacks.

Dredge, S. (2014) Barcroft Media Aims for a Killing with Videos that Grab Digital Natives, *Guardian*, 11 May, www.theguardian.com/media/2014/may/11/barcroft-media-short-form-videos-youtube.

Economist, The (2009) The Internet's Librarian, *The Economist*, **390** (8621), 34.

Economist, The (2010) The Data Deluge, *The Economist*, **394** (8671), 11.

Economist, The (2011) A New, Improved Hit Machine: discovering musical talent, *The Economist*, **401** (8756), 84.

Economist, The (2014) Media Firms Are Making Big Bets on Online Video, Still an Untested Medium, *The Economist*, 3 May, www.economist.com/news/business/21601558-media-firms-are-making-big-bets-online-video-still-untested-medium-newtube.

Fehrenbacher, K. (2011) *Cool Finnish Weather the New Hotness for Data Centers*, GigaOm, 12 September, http://gigaom.com/cleantech/cool-finnish-weather-the-new-hotness-for-green-data-centers.

Fenez, M. and van der Donk, M. (2010) *From Paper to Platform: transforming the B2B publishing business model*, PricewaterhouseCoopers, www.pwc.com/gx/en/entertainment-media/pdf/the-future-of-B2B-publishing.pdf.

Firmstone, J. and Coleman, S. (2014) The Changing Role of the Local News Media in Enabling Citizens to Engage in Local Democracies, *Journalism Practice*, **8** (5), http://dx.doi.org/10.1080/17512786.2014.895516.

Flickr (2014) *Explore Creative Commons*, www.flickr.com/creativecommons/.

Flood, A. (2014) Bookless Library Opened by New US University, *Guardian*, 29 August, www.theguardian.com/books/2014/aug/29/bookless-library-new-us-university-florida-polytechnic-digital.

Foucault, M. (1977) *Discipline and Punish: the birth of the prison*, Allen Lane.

Fuchs, C. et al. (eds) (2012) *Internet and Surveillance: the challenges of Web 2.0 and social media*, Routledge.

Gapper, J. (2014) Silicon Valley Gets Excited about a Small News Story, *Financial Times*, 9 April, www.ft.com/cms/s/0/f459bca4-bf29-11e3-a4af-00144feabdc0.html#axzz38O2Djpgh.

Gartner (2014) *Gartner Says Annual Smartphone Sales Surpassed Sales of Feature Phones for the First Time in 2013*, press release, 13 February, www.gartner.com/newsroom/id/2665715.

Gertner, J. (2014) Can Jeff Immelt really make the world 1% better?, *Fast Company*, July/August, 70–8.

Gibson, A. (2010) *Local By Social: how local authorities can use social media to achieve more for less*, www.idea.gov.uk/idk/aio/17801438.

Giddens, A. (1990) *The Consequences of Modernity*, Polity Press.

Graham, G. and Hill, J. (2009) The Regional Newspaper Industry Value Chain in the Digital Age, *OR Insight*, **22**, 165–83.

Greenslade, R. (2013) Lloyd's List, the World's Oldest Newspaper, to Give up on

Print, *Guardian*, 25 September, www.theguardian.com/media/greenslade/2013/
sep/25/newspapers-digital-media.

Greenwald, G. (2013) XKeyscore: NSA tool collects 'nearly everything a user does
on the internet', *Guardian*, 31 July, www.theguardian.com/world/2013/jul/31/
nsa-top-secret-program-online-data.

Hall, K. (2011) Public Data Could Boost the Economy but Whose Information Is It
Anyway?, *Computer Weekly*, 6 December, 4.

Halliday, J. (2010) ISPs Should Be Free to Abandon Net Neutrality, says Ed Vaizey,
Guardian, 17 November,
www.guardian.co.uk/technology/2010/nov/17/net-neutrality-ed-vaizey.

Harris, R. (2009) *Long-term Personal Data Storage*, ZDNet, 4 January,
www.zdnet.com/blog/storage/long-term-personal-data-storage/376.

Hemp, P. (2009) Death by Information Overload, *Harvard Business Review*, **87** (9),
82–9.

Henry, N. (1974) Knowledge Management: a new concern for public administration,
Public Administration Review, **34** (3), 189–96.

Herrman, J. and Buchanan, M. (2010) *The Future of Storage*, Gizmodo, 19 March,
http://gizmodo.com/5497512/the-future-of-storage.

Hill, K. (2011) Yes, the CIA's 'Ninja Librarians' Are Tracking Twitter and Facebook
(As They Should), *Forbes*, 9 November,
www.forbes.com/sites/kashmirhill/2011/11/09/yes-the-cias-ninja-librarians-are-
tracking-twitter-and-facebook-as-they-should/.

Hitchcock, G. (2011) British Museum Makes the Wikipedia Connection, *Guardian*,
8 August, www.guardian.co.uk/government-computing-network/2011/aug/08/
british-museum-wikipedia.

Hodson, H. (2014) Google's Fact-Checking Bots Build Vast Knowledge Bank, *New
Scientist*, 20 August, www.newscientist.com/article/mg22329832.700-googles-
factchecking-bots-build-vast-knowledge-bank.html#.VA1t_PldUXo.

Howard, E. (2014) E-petitions Can be Very Effective, but Don't Put Them in the
Hands of Government, *Guardian*, 24 February, www.theguardian.com/
commentisfree/2014/feb/24/e-petitions-often-worse-than-useless.

Howard, P. et al. (2011) *Opening Closed Regimes: what was the role of social media during
the Arab Spring?*, University of Washington, http://pitpi.org/wp-content/
uploads/2013/02/2011_Howard-Duffy-Freelon-Hussain-Mari-Mazaid_pITPI.pdf.

Hyams, E. (2011a) Making Sense of the World with Ranganathan and a Fluffy Toy,
CILIP Update, September, 21–3.

Hyams, E. (2011b) What's New in the Econtent Market?, *CILIP Update*, November,
37–40.

IDC (2013) *New IDC Worldwide Big Data Technology and Services Forecast Shows Market
Expected to Grow to $32.4 Billion in 2017*, International Data Corporation,
www.idc.com/getdoc.jsp?containerId=prUS24542113.

IDC (2014) *Smartphone OS Market Share, Q2 2014*, International Data Corporation, www.idc.com/prodserv/smartphone-os-market-share.jsp.

Internet Archive (2014) *About the Internet Archive*, www.archive.org/about/about.php.

Isenberg, D. (1998) The Dawn of the Stupid Network, *ACM netWorker*, **2** (1), 24–31.

Jackson, J. (2010) Google: 129 million different books have been published, *PC World*, 6 August, www.pcworld.com/article/202803/google_129_million_different_books_ have_been_published.html.

Jarvis, J. (2009) *What Would Google Do?*, Collins.

Jurkowitz, M. (2014) *The Growth in Digital Reporting: what it means for journalism and news consumers*, PewResearch Journalism Project, 26 March, www.journalism.org/2014/03/26/the-growth-in-digital-reporting/.

Kidd, A. (2003) Document Retention: the IT manager's changing role, *TechRepublic*, 28 July, www.techrepublic.com/article/document-retention-the-it-managers-changingrole/5054924.

King, E. (2010) *Free for All: the internet's transformation of journalism*, Northwestern University Press.

Kiss, J. (2014) Academics: UK 'Drip' data law changes are 'serious expansion of surveillance', *Guardian*, 15 July, www.theguardian.com/technology/2014/jul/15/academics-uk-data-law-surveillance-bill-rushed-parliament.

Knopper, S. (2009) *Appetite for Self-destruction: the spectacular crash of the record industry in the digital age*, Free Press.

Komorowski, M. (2014) *A History of Storage Cost*, www.mkomo.com/cost-per-gigabyte-update.

Lanier, J. (2013) *Who Owns the Future?*, Allen Lane.

Lee, D. (2014) *Apple's iPod: is the end nigh?*, BBC News, 29 January, www.bbc.co.uk/news/technology-25927366.

Lee, M. and Lan, Y. (2007) From Web 2.0 to Conversational Knowledge: towards collaborative intelligence, *Journal of Entrepreneurship Research*, **2** (2), 47–62.

Lehrer, J. (2010) Our Cluttered Minds, *New York Times*, 3 June, www.nytimes.com/2010/06/06/books/review/Lehrer-t.html.

Leiner, B. et al. (2009) A Brief History of the Internet, *ACM SIGCOMM Computer Communication Review*, **39** (5), 22–31.

Leonhard, W. (2014) Microsoft Allegedly Paying Bloggers to Promote IE, *InfoWorld*, 18 June, www.infoworld.com/t/web-browsers/microsoft-allegedly-paying-bloggers-promote-ie-244557.

Lesk, M. (1997) *How Much Information Is There In the World?*, www.lesk.com/mlesk/ksg97/ksg.html.

Lessig, L. (2004) *Free Culture*, The Penguin Press.

Levie, A. (2011) *The Smarter Enterprise*, http://gigaom.com/collaboration/the-smarter-enterprise.

Levy, M. (2009) Web 2.0 Implications on Knowledge Management, *Journal of Knowledge Management*, **13** (1), 120–34.

Lewis, M. (2014) *Flash Boys*, Allen Lane.

Libbenga, J. (2011) Sweden Postpones EU Data Retention Directive, Faces Court, Fines, *The Register*, 18 March, www.theregister.co.uk/2011/03/18/sweden_postpones_eu_data_retention_directive/.

Luckhurst, T. (2011) Black and White and Dead All Over?, *Times Higher Education*, 8 September, 38.

Lyman, P. and Varian, H. R. (2000) How Much Information?, *Journal of Electronic Publishing*, **6** (2).

Lyman, P. and Varian, H. R. (2003) *How Much Information?*, www2.sims.berkeley.edu/research/projects/how-much-info-2003.

Lynch, C. (2003) Institutional Repositories: essential infrastructure for scholarship in the digital age, *ARL Bimonthly Report*, 226.

Machlup, F. (1962) *The Production and Distribution of Knowledge in the United States*, Princeton University Press.

MailOnline (2014) *Global Statistics*, http://mailconnected.co.uk/uploads/files/MailOnline-Summary.pdf.

Mandel, M. (2012) *Beyond Goods and Services: the (unmeasured) rise of the data-driven economy*, Progressive Policy Institute, www.progressivepolicy.org/slider/beyond-goods-and-services-the-unmeasured-rise-of-the-data-driven-economy/.

Manyika, J. and Roxburgh, C. (2011) *The Great Transformer: the impact of the internet on economic growth and prosperity*, McKinsey Global Institute, www.mckinsey.com/Insights/MGI/Research/Technology_and_Innovation/The_great_transformer.

Manyika, J. et al. (2011) *Big Data: the next frontier for innovation, competition, and productivity*, McKinsey Global Institute, www.mckinsey.com/Insights/MGI/Research/Technology_and_Innovation/Big_data_The_next_frontier_for_innovation.

Mason, R. (2014) Right to be Forgotten: Wikipedia chief enters internet censorship row, *Guardian*, 25 July, www.theguardian.com/technology/2014/jul/25/right-to-be-forgotten-google-wikipedia-jimmy-wales.

Mason Williams (2014) *UK Bloggers More Commercially Savvy than their European Counterparts*, www.mason-williams.co.uk/2014/06/uk-bloggers-commercially-savvy-european-counterparts/.

Maxcer, C. (2007) Fail-Safe System Fails in Alaska's Data Debacle, *Tech News World*, 21 March, www.technewsworld.com/rsstory/56414.html.

McAfee, A. (2009) *Enterprise 2.0: new collaborative tools for your organization's toughest challenges*, Harvard Business School Press.

McCandless, D. (2010) *How Much Do Music Artists Earn Online?*, Information is Beautiful, 13 April, www.informationisbeautiful.net/2010/how-much-do-music-artists-earn-online/.

Miller, C. and Bilton, N. (2011) Google's Lab of Wildest Dreams, *New York Times*, 13 November, www.nytimes.com/2011/11/14/technology/at-google-x-a-top-secret-lab-dreaming-up-the-future.html?pagewanted=all.

Miller, R. (2011) *Report: Google uses about 900,000 servers*, Data Center Knowledge, www.datacenterknowledge.com/archives/2011/08/01/report-google-uses-about-900000-servers.

Miller, R. (2013) *Iron Mountain is Taking the Data Center Underground, Data Center Knowledge*, www.datacenterknowledge.com/archives/2013/05/08/iron-mountain/.

Mitchell, A. et al. (2013) *The Role of News on Facebook*, PewResearch Journalism Project, 24 October, www.journalism.org/2013/10/24/the-role-of-news-on-facebook/.

Morozov, E. (2011) *The Net Delusion: how not to liberate the world*, Penguin.

Mountain Complex, The (n.d.) *Unsurpassed Security*, www.omuvs.com/dataCenter/.

National Archives (2011) *The United Kingdom Report on the Re-use of Public Sector Information*, www.nationalarchives.gov.uk/documents/information-management/psi-report.pdf.

Newton, M., Miller, C. and Stowell Bracke, M. (2011) Librarian Roles in Institutional Repository Data Set Collecting: outcomes of a research library task force, *Collection Management*, **36** (1), 53–67.

Nonaka, I. and Takeuchi, H. (1995) *The Knowledge Creating Company: how Japanese companies create the dynasties of innovation*, Oxford University Press.

OECD (2010) *The Evolution of News and the Internet*, Organisation for Economic Cooperation and Development, www.oecd.org/dataoecd/30/24/45559596.pdf.

OECD (2014) *OECD Broadband Statistics Update*, Organisation for Economic Co-operation and Development, www.oecd.org/internet/broadband/broadband-statistics-update.htm.

Ofcom (2013) *Media Literacy Data*.

Ofcom (2014) *Communications Market Report*.

ONS (2014) *Internet Access 2014*, Office for National Statistics, www.ons.gov.uk/ons/rel/rdit2/internet-access-quarterly-update-q1-2014/ index.html.

Pang, B. and Lee, L. (2008) Opinion Mining and Sentiment Analysis, *Foundations and Trends in Information Retrieval*, **2** (1–2), 1–135.

Pariser, E. (2011) *The Filter Bubble: what the internet is hiding from you*, Viking.

Perez, S. (2014) iTunes App Store Now Has 1.2 Million Apps, Has Seen 75 Billion Downloads To Date, *TechCrunch*, 2 June, http://techcrunch.com/2014/06/02/itunes-app-store-now-has-1-2-million-apps-has-seen-75-billion-downloads-to-date/.

Phillips, H. (2010) The Great Library of Alexandria?, *Library Philosophy and Practice*, August.

PIRA (2000) *Commercial Exploitation of Europe's Public Sector Information*, PIRA International.

Prithviraj, K. and Kumar, B. (2014) Corrosion of URLs: implications for electronic publishing, *IFLA Journal*, **40** (1), 35–47.

Purcell, A. (2013) *Data in the DNA: transforming biology and data storage*, International Science Grid This Week, 9 October, www.isgtw.org/feature/data-dna-transforming-biology-and-data-storage.

Quah, D. (1996) *The Invisible Hand and the Weightless Economy*, Centre for Economic Performance occasional papers, CEPOP12, Centre for Economic Performance, London School of Economics and Political Science.

Radicati Group (2013) *Email Statistics Report 2013–17*, www.radicati.com/wp/wp-content/uploads/2013/04/Email-Statistics-Report-2013-2017-Executive-Summary.pdf.

Rao, P. (2014) The Top Fashion Bloggers Making Millions Aren't Who You Think, *Vanity Fair*, June, www.vanityfair.com/online/daily/2014/06/fashion-bloggers-making-millions.

Rosenbloom, S. (2007) On Facebook, Scholars Link Up With Data, *New York Times*, 17 December, www.nytimes.com/2007/12/17/style/17facebook.html?_r=2&sq=d.

Rossini, C. (2010) British Library Indicates Shift to Digital, *Guardian*, 20 September, https://groups.google.com/forum/#!topic/rea-lista/fz4gTe2r9l8.

Roth, D. (2009) The Answer Factory: Demand Media and the fast, disposable, and profitable as hell media model, *Wired*, October, www.wired.com/2009/10/ff_demandmedia/.

Ryan, T. (2013) Sears Replaces Retail Stores With Data Centers, *Forbes*, 31 May, www.forbes.com/sites/retailwire/2013/05/31/sears-replaces-retail-stores-with-data-centers/.

Sandvine (2014) *Global Internet Phenomena Report*, www.sandvine.com/downloads/general/global-internet-phenomena/2014/1h-2014-global-internet-phenomena-report.pdf.

Schumpeter, J. (1950) *Capitalism, Socialism, and Democracy*, 3rd edn, Harper.

Scoble, R. and Israel, S. (2006) *Naked Conversations: how blogs are changing the way businesses talk with customers*, John Wiley and Sons.

SCONUL (1999) *Information Skills in Higher Education: a SCONUL position paper*, www.sconul.ac.uk/groups/information_literacy/seven_pillars.html.

Shakespeare, S. (2013) *An Independent Review of Public Sector Information*, www.gov.uk/government/publications/shakespeare-review-of-public-sector-information.

Shapiro, C. and Varian, H. (1999) *Information Rules*, Harvard Business School Press.

Shirky, C. (2008) *Here Comes Everybody*, Allen Lane.

Simon, S. and Will, M. (2013) *Textbook Publishers Revamp E-books to Fight Used Market*, Reuters, 23 July, www.reuters.com/article/2013/07/23/us-usa-education-textbook-idUSBRE96M04520130723.

Simonite, T. (2014) The Decline of Wikipedia, *MIT Technology Review*, **116**, (6), 51–6.

Stevenson, V. and Hodges, S. (2008) Setting up a University Digital Repository: experience with DigiTool, *OCLC Systems and Services: international digital library perspectives*, **24** (1), 48–50.

Stonier, T. (1983) *The Wealth of Information*, Thames Methuen.

Sullivan, A. (2009) The Revolution will be Twittered, *The Atlantic*, 13 June, www.theatlantic.com/daily-dish/archive/2009/06/the-revolution-will-be-twittered/200478/.

Sullivan D. (2012a) *Google's Jaw-Dropping Sponsored Post Campaign for Chrome*, Search Engine Land, 2 January, http://searchengineland.com/googles-jaw-dropping-sponsored-post-campaign-for-chrome-106348.

Sullivan, D. (2012b) *Google: 100 billion searches per month, search to integrate Gmail, launching enhanced search app for iOS*, Search Engine Land, 8 August, http://searchengineland.com/google-search-press-129925.

Sullivan, D. (2014) *The Yahoo Directory — once the Internet's Most Important Search Engine — is to Close*, Search Engine Land, 26 September, http://searchengineland.com/yahoo-directory-close-204370.

Sverdlik, Y. (2014) *Apple Data Center Energy Use Grows but Remains 100 Percent Renewable*, Data Center Knowledge, www.datacenterknowledge.com/archives/2014/07/17/apple-data-center-energy-use-grows-remains-100-percent-renewable/.

Sweney, M. (2014) Mail Online Ad Revenue up 51%, *Guardian*, 27 March, www.theguardian.com/media/2014/mar/27/mail-online-ad-revenue-misses-target.

Thurman, N. and Rodgers, J. (2014). Citizen Journalism in Real Time: live blogging and crisis events. In Thorsen, E. and Allan, S. (eds), *Citizen Journalism: global perspectives*, Peter Lang.

Toffler, A. (1970) *Future Shock*, Bodley Head.

Toffler, A. (1980) *The Third Wave*, Bantam Books.

Toffler, A. (1990) *Powershift: knowledge, wealth and violence at the edge of the 21st century*, Bantam Books.

Transparency Market Research (2013) *Personal and Entry Level Storage (PELS) Market – global industry analysis, size, share, growth, trends and forecast*, www.transparencymarketresearch.com/personal-entry-level-storage.html.

Tumblr (2014) Tumblr at a Glance, www.tumblr.com/about.

Turgeman, Y., Alm, E. and Ratti, C. (2014) Smart Toilets and Sewer Sensors Are Coming, *Wired*, March, **56**.

Turner, V. et al. (2014) *The Digital Universe of Opportunities: rich data and the increasing value of the internet of things*, IDC, http://idcdocserv.com/1678.

University of Virginia Library (2011) *AIMS – Born Digital Collections: an inter-institutional model for stewardship*, www2.lib.virginia.edu/aims.

Vierstraete, M. (2014) ECJ Declares the Data Retention Directive to be Invalid:

what's next?, *Olswang Legal and Regulatory News*, www.olswang.com/articles/
2014/04/ecjdeclaresthedataretentiondirectivetobeinvalidwhat%E2%80%99s-next/.

Wagner, K. (2013) *Facebook has a Quarter of a Trillion User Photos*, Mashable, 17
September, http://mashable.com/2013/09/16/facebook-photo-uploads/.

Waibel, G. (2014) *About Smithsonian X 3D*, http://3d.si.edu/about.

WAN-IFRA (2014) *World Press Trends*, World Association of Newspapers and News
Publishers, http://blog.wan-ifra.org/2014/06/09/world-press-trends-print-and-
digital-together-increasing-newspaper-audiences.

Wang, M. (2007) Introducing CRM into an Academic Library, *Library Management*,
28 (6/7), 281–91.

Wardle, C., Dubberley, S. and Brown, P. (2014) *Amateur Footage: a global study of user-
generated content in TV and online news output*, Tow Centre for Digital Journalism,
Columbia Journalism School, http://usergeneratednews.towcenter.org/
wp-content/uploads/2014/05/Tow-Center-UGC-Report.pdf.

Watson Hall (2014) *UK Data Retention Requirements*, https://www.watsonhall.com/
resources/downloads/paper-uk-data-retention-requirements.pdf.

Waxman, L. et al. (2007) The Library as Place: providing students with opportunities
for socialization, relaxation, and restoration, *New Library World*, **108** (9/10),
424–34.

Wells, M. (2011) How Live Blogging Has Transformed Journalism, *Guardian*, 28
March, www.theguardian.com/media/2011/mar/28/live-blogging-transforms-
journalism.

White, A. (2014) *Google Jogs Memories Meant to Be Forgotten, Watchdog Says*,
Bloomberg, 24 July, www.bloomberg.com/news/2014-07-23/google-jogs-
memories-meant-to-be-forgotten-watchdog-says.html.

WikiLeaks (n.d.) *What is WikiLeaks?*, https://wikileaks.org/About.html.

Wikipedia (2013) About, www.wikipedia.org/wiki/about.

Williams, C. (2011) How Egypt Shut Down the Internet, *Telegraph*, 28 January,
www.telegraph.co.uk/news/worldnews/africaandindianocean/egypt/8288163/
How-Egypt-shut-down-the-internet.html.

Williams, M. (2005) *Gale Directory of Databases*, Gale Group.

Wilson, T. (2002) The Nonsense of Knowledge Management, *Information Research*,
8 (1).

Woodward, H. and Estelle, L. (2010) *Digital Information: order or anarchy?*, Facet
Publishing.

WordPress (2014) http://en.wordpress.com/stats/.

YouTube (2014) Statistics, www.youtube.com/yt/press/en-GB/statistics.html.

Zittrain, J. (2008) *The Future of the Internet*, Yale University Press.

Index